CROCHET ICONIC WOMEN

Amigurumi Patterns for 15 Women Who Changed the World

CARLA MITRANI

BY BUYING THIS BOOK YOU ARE HELPING TO SUPPORT

WONDER
FOUNDATION

CROCHET
ICONIC
WOMEN

CONTENTS

FOREWORD

Not long ago, crochet was considered outdated and traditional in a negative sense of the word, between potholders and crochet doilies and, to be honest, it was rarely associated with the self-determined modern image of women.

And yet it is just that!

Perception has changed and crochet has rediscovered itself, just like all the brave women in this book who impressively demonstrate that it's possible to break through dusty thought patterns, reinvent yourself and remain true to yourself nevertheless. Modern role models for generations of subsequent women and girls.

We owe the concentrated yarn-incarnate emancipation gathered in this book to the wonderful Carla Mitrani, who loves and lives all the contradictions of a modern woman and goes her own way with this fabulous book.

Just as Audrey Hepburn said: "Nothing is impossible, the word itself says 'I'm possible'!"

Lydia Tresselt

Lydia Tresselt is the talented designer behind the Lalylala brand of crochet patterns, and the author of Beetles, Bugs and Butterflies www.lalylala.com

ICONS

WELCOME!

Hello my fellow crocheters and friends! It's a real pleasure to welcome you to this collection of crochet tributes to some of the most extraordinary women who have shaped our present or who are currently building our future.

Of course, we had to narrow the list down to 15 dolls and I am sure you will find that many are missing (Crochet Iconic Women Vol. 2, maybe?), but this is just a starting point; I strongly believe that the lives of these ladies are representative of the power of women and will be an endless source of inspiration. However, I wish that they should not only be taken as examples of successes and triumphs but mostly as stories of resilience, of overcoming impossible obstacles in the quest of the most amazing dreams.

The women in this book were not perfect but, with their complexities and flaws, they were all visionaries, brave, talented, smart, courageous and strong. Some of them had minds ahead of their time by many decades. Others sparked movements that became global and gave a voice to the voiceless.

I would love to see these dolls decorating your room or workplace, so whenever you look at them, they can be a reminder of what can be accomplished when one dares to dream. Or I hope you crochet them for little ones to play with and thus start the conversation about their extraordinary and influential lives. By the end of the book I am sure you will be able to include some modifications to the patterns, make hair curls longer or shorter and change the colours or skin tones to create your own special icons.

So let's grab hooks and yarns and start crocheting!

Carla

TOOLS AND MATERIALS

HOOKS AND YARNS

All the dolls in this book were crocheted using a 2.5mm (US C/2) crochet hook and 8-ply DK weight cotton yarn. I crochet really tightly, which is important so that holes are not created and the fibrefill toy stuffing won't show through the stitches. If you tend to crochet a bit looser, then you should probably choose a smaller hook.

I only use 100% cotton yarns because I like the feel and finish of cotton; it runs smoothly in your hands when working and it will not pill as acrylic or woollen yarns do, which makes these dolls more durable when intended for children. Cotton also builds a sturdier fabric for stuffed dolls, which will not stretch and will hold the stuffing better, without distorting the shapes and volumes of the bodies.

Crochet hooks

Sizes 2.5mm (US C/2) and 2mm (US B/1). The smaller hook is needed to crochet Jane Goodall's little chimpanzee friend Flint, and for Marie Curie's Erlenmeyer Flask and Florence Nightingale's lamp.

Cotton yarn

8-ply DK weight 100% soft cotton. I worked with the following yarn by Hobbii:

8/8 Rainbow Cotton

• Fibre: 100% soft cotton

• Ball weight: 50g (1.8oz)

• Length: 75m (82yds)

• Yarn weight: DK (light worsted)

For Jane's friend Flint, Marie Curie's Erlenmeyer Flask and Florence's Lamp I worked with the following yarn, also by Hobbii:

8/4 Rainbow Cotton

• Fibre: 100% soft cotton

• Ball weight: 50g (1.8oz)

• Length: 170m (186yds)

• Yarn weight: Fingering (super fine)

How much yarn is needed?

One of the best things about making the dolls in this book is that none of them uses an entire 50g ball of yarn. In fact, you can use one ball of skin colour to make two dolls. So save all your leftovers and scraps, because they can become skirts, purses or hats!

OTHER TOOLS AND MATERIALS

Toy safety eyes

Plastic, black, size 8mm (1/3in) for the dolls and 6mm (1/4in) for Flint, Jane Goodall's chimpanzee friend.

For safety reasons, if you are planning to give the doll to a small child, you should embroider the eyes using black, dark grey or brown yarn instead.

Stuffing

Polyester fibrefill stuffing – you will need to stuff firmly!

Scissors and seam ripper

Sometimes we just need to unravel and start over and there is nothing wrong with that!

Stitch markers

When crocheting in a spiral, it's important to mark the beginning of each round with a stitch marker and move this stitch marker up as you work. You can use paper clips, hair clips or safety pins too.

Tapestry/yarn needle

Use this to sew the arms, hair and other accessories to your dolls. Find one with a blunted tip, so it won't split the yarn and with an eye big enough to fit your choice of yarn.

Pins

These can be very helpful to hold certain pieces, like hairbuns, while you sew them. Choose those with coloured plastic or beaded heads so they won't slip inside the doll. Ouch!

Wooden chopstick

This is the secret weapon – there is nothing better than a broken chopstick to evenly spread the stuffing in complicated, hard to reach places!

Craft bag and pencil case

The best thing about crochet is that you can take your current project everywhere! So be ready to pack your hooks, needles and yarns and continue your work in waiting rooms, on public transportation or in parks!

STITCHES

STITCH ABBREVIATIONS

The patterns in this book are written using US crochet terms. These are listed here, along with their UK equivalents (where applicable):

ch = chain stitch

slst = slip stitch

sc = single crochet (UK double crochet)

sc2tog = single crochet 2 stitches together (UK double crochet 2 stitches together)

hdc = half double crochet (UK half treble crochet)

dc = double crochet (UK treble crochet)

FLO = front loop only

BLO = back loop only

beg = beginning

rep = repeat

approx = approximately

* = denotes the beginning of a repeat sequence. Repeat the instructions that follow the * as instructed

STITCHES USED

SLIP KNOT

The slip knot is the starting point of the foundation chain and it does not count as a stitch. Make a loop shape with the tail end of the yarn. Insert the hook into it, yarn over hook and draw another loop through it. Pull the yarn tail to tighten the loop around the hook.

CHAIN STITCH (CH)

Start with a slip knot, then yarn over hook and pull through the loop on your hook to create one chain stitch. Repeat this as many times as stated in your pattern.

SLIP STITCH (SLST)

Insert your hook into the stitch, yarn over hook and pull through the stitch and the loop on the hook at the same time.

SINGLE CROCHET (SC)

Insert the hook into the stitch, yarn over hook and pull the yarn back through the stitch. You will now have two loops on the hook. Yarn over again and draw it through both loops at once.

HALF DOUBLE CROCHET (HDC)

Yarn over hook and then insert your hook into the stitch, yarn over hook and pull the yarn through the stitch (you will have three loops on the hook). Yarn over hook and pull through all three loops on the hook in one go.

DOUBLE CROCHET (DC)

Yarn over hook and insert your hook into the stitch, yarn over hook and pull the yarn through the stitch (you will have three loops on the hook). Yarn over hook and pull through the first two loops on the hook in one go (this will leave two loops remaining on the hook). Yarn over hook one last time and draw through the last two remaining loops on the hook.

SINGLE CROCHET 2 STITCHES TOGETHER (SC2TOG)

Working two stitches together creates a decrease of one stitch, and for the dolls in this book the single crochet decrease (sc2tog) is worked as an invisible decrease. See *Techniques: Invisible Single Crochet Decrease* for detailed instructions and photos.

PICOT STITCH (PICOT ST)

Make three chain stitches. Then crochet one sc in the first of those chain stitches (third chain from hook).

SURFACE SINGLE CROCHET (SURFACE SC)

This is the stitch I use to create the 'V' of the collar *(see Techniques: Creating the V Collar)*. After joining yarn as indicated in your pattern, work regular single crochet stitches but instead of working into the top part of a stitch, you will work over the body of the doll, through the spaces in between the stitches, by inserting your hook down into the first space then up and out through the next space along, then complete your single crochet as usual.

BOBBLE STITCH (BOBBLE ST)

This is the stitch I use to create the nose of the dolls. If you don't want to use this stitch, you can embroider the nose using the same yarn and your tapestry needle. The bobble stitch is a cluster of unfinished dc stitches worked into one stitch, achieved by leaving the last loop of each dc on the hook, to close them all together at the end. Work a bobble stitch by following these step-by-step instructions:

Yarn over hook (**1**) and insert the hook into the stitch. Yarn over hook again and draw the yarn through the stitch. You now have three loops on the hook (**2**). Yarn over hook again and pull it through the first two loops on the hook (**3**). You now have one unfinished double crochet stitch and two loops remain on the hook.

In the same stitch, repeat the previous steps four more times, to create four more unfinished double crochet stitches into that stitch. You must end with six loops on your hook (**4**).

Finally, yarn over hook and draw through all six loops on the hook at once, to create the cluster (**5**).

If, after finishing, you end up with the bump protruding from the wrong side of the fabric (**6**), just push it towards the outside to build the nose (**7**).

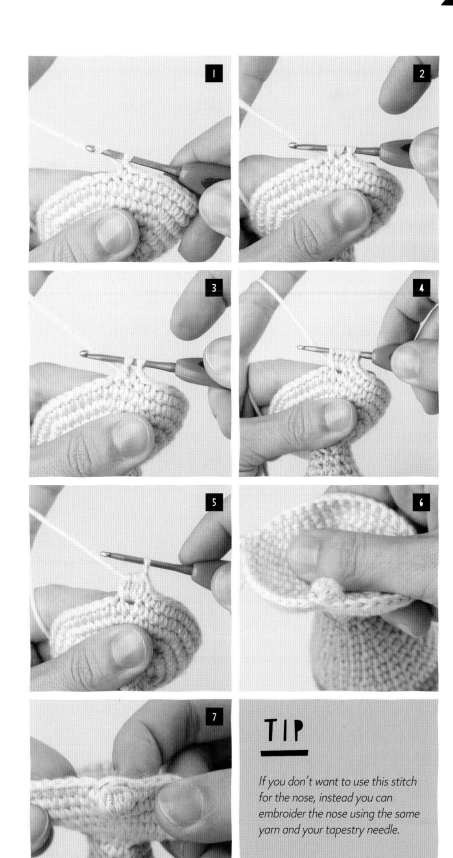

TIP

If you don't want to use this stitch for the nose, instead you can embroider the nose using the same yarn and your tapestry needle.

PROJECTS

MATERIALS

2.5mm (C/2) crochet hook

100% 8-ply cotton; colours used: skin colour, white, beige, light brown, dark brown, mustard, small amount of pink

Yarn needle

8mm (⅓in) safety eyes

Stitch marker

Fibrefill stuffing

FINISHED SIZE

20cm (7¾in) tall

AMELIA EARHART

Why Amelia? Because she was a passionate and fearless chaser of dreams, who never gave up, in spite of the enormous challenges she faced in achieving her dreams. She wanted to fly and she flew. She wanted to cross the Atlantic Ocean with her plane, and she did. She dared to go where no other woman had gone before and encouraged others to follow her example of bravery. She was confident in the true power of women, knowing they could also excel in their chosen professions. And even though she died in the pursuit of her greatest feat, she still remains a guiding light for all like-minded dreamers.

LEG 1

Round 1: Using **light brown** for the boots, 6 sc in a magic ring. (6 sts)

Round 2: 2 sc in each st. (12 sts)

Rounds 3 to 6: 1 sc in each st.

Round 7: Change to **beige** for the pants, 1 sc BLO in each st.

Rounds 8 and 9: 1 sc in each st. Fasten off. Set aside.

LEG 2

Work as for Leg 1, but do not fasten off yarn at the end. We will continue with the body.

BODY

Round 10: Still with leg 2 on your hook, ch 3 and join to leg 1 with a sc *(see Techniques: Joining Legs)*, place a stitch marker here for new beg of round, work 11 sc all along leg 1, 1 sc into each ch of 3-ch-loop, 12 sc all along leg 2 and 1 sc into other side of each ch of 3-ch-loop. (30 sts)

Round 11: *4 sc, 2 sc in the next st, rep from * to end. (36 sts)

Rounds 12 to 15: 1 sc in each st.

Round 16: Change to **light brown** for the belt, 1 sc BLO in each st.

Round 17: *4 sc, sc2tog, rep from * to end. (30 sts)

Round 18: Change to **white** for the shirt, 1 sc BLO in each st.

Rounds 19 and 20: 1 sc in each st.

Stuff the legs firmly at this point.

Round 21: *3 sc, sc2tog, rep from * to end. (24 sts)

Rounds 22 and 23: 1 sc in each st.

Round 24: *2 sc, sc2tog, rep from * to end. (18 sts)

Stuff the body firmly at this point.

Rounds 25 and 26: 1 sc in each st.

Round 27: *1 sc, sc2tog, rep from * to end. (12 sts)

Round 28: 1 sc in each st.

Round 29: / sc, change to **skin** colour, 1 sc, change back to **white**, 4 sc.

Round 30: 6 sc, change to **skin** colour, 3 sc, change back to **white**, 3 sc.

Round 31: 5 sc, change to **skin** colour, 5 sc, change back to **white**, 2 sc.

You should have a **skin** colour triangle at the front centre of the doll.

Do not fasten off yarn. We will continue with the head.

HEAD

Round 32: Change to **skin** colour, 2 sc BLO in each of the first 5 sts (those in **white**), 2 sc through both loops in each of the following 5 sts (those in **skin** colour), 2 sc BLO in each of last 2 sts (those in **white**). (24 sts)

Round 33: *3 sc, 2 sc in the next st, rep from * to end. (30 sts)

Stuff the neck area firmly at this point.

Round 34: *4 sc, 2 sc in the next st, rep from * to end. (36 sts)

Round 35: *5 sc, 2 sc in the next st, rep from * to end. (42 sts)

Round 36: 1 sc in each st.

Round 37: 27 sc, 1 bobble st for the nose *(see Stitches: Bobble st)*, 1 sc in each st to end.

Be sure to align the nose with the middle of the legs, and the **skin** colour triangle at the neck, and adjust the positioning if necessary.

We will take a break here from the head to work the collar of Amelia's shirt. Place a stitch marker in the loop on your hook to secure.

For detailed photographs of how to work a collar see *Techniques: Creating the V Collar.*

Join the **white** yarn 2 rounds below the tip of the **skin** triangle.

Work in the spaces between stitches and crochet 2 surface sc up until you reach the bottom tip of the triangle.

Now follow the diagonal of the triangle, working the right side first. Crochet 1 surface sc in between each round, inserting the hook in the spaces between rounds, until you reach the round where the white front loops are showing.

Now crochet 2 sc in each front loop of the shirt bordering Amelia's neck, until you reach the edge of the triangle on the other side. (14 sts). Work 5 surface sc in between rounds following the diagonal of the triangle to the starting stitch, work 1 slst in the starting stitch. Fasten off and weave in ends.

We will now continue with the head. Rejoin the **skin** colour yarn to where you stopped working the head.

Rounds 38 to 46: 1 sc in each st.

Round 47: *5 sc, sc2tog, rep from * to end. (36 sts)

Start stuffing the head at this point.

Round 48: *4 sc, sc2tog, rep from * to end. (30 sts)

Place safety eyes one round above the nose, with 8 sts between them, embroider cheeks with **pink** yarn.

Round 49: *3 sc, sc2tog, rep from * to end. (24 sts)

Round 50: *2 sc, sc2tog, rep from * to end. (18 sts)
Stuff firmly.

Round 51: *1 sc, sc2tog, rep from * to end. (12 sts)

Round 52: (sc2tog) 6 times. (6 sts)
Fasten off and weave in ends.

ARMS (MAKE TWO)

Round 1: Using **skin** colour, ch 2, 4 sc in the second ch from hook. (4 sts)

Round 2: 2 sc in each st. (8 sts)

Rounds 3 to 5: 1 sc in each st.

Round 6: Change to **mustard** yarn for the jacket, 1 sc BLO in each st.

Rounds 7 to 17: 1 sc in each st. There is no need to stuff the arms.

Round 18: Press the opening with your fingers, aligning 4 sts side by side and sc both sides together by working 1 sc into each pair of sts *(see Techniques: Closing the Arms)*.

Fasten off, leaving a long tail to sew to the body.

TIP

If you don't want to do Amelia's collar with surface single crochet, just embroider two diagonal lines using the colour of her shirt, to mark the edges of the skin triangle showing on her neck.

"Please know I am quite aware of the hazards. I want to do it because I want to do it. Women must try to do things as men have tried. When they fail, their failure must be but a challenge to others."

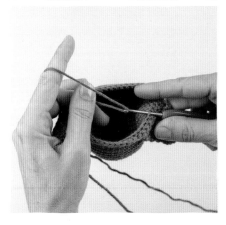

JACKET

The jacket is actually a vest, but when you put it on your Amelia, together with the arms, it will look like a jacket. The vest is worked in rows, using **mustard**.

Row 1: Ch 21, 1 sc in the second ch from hook, 1 sc in each ch to end, ch 1, turn. (20 sc)

Row 2: 4 sc, *ch 6, skip the following 4 sts (to create armhole), 4 sc, rep from * once more, ch 1, turn.

Row 3: 4 sc, *6 sc in the 6-ch-loop, 4 sc, rep from * once more, ch 1, turn. (24 sts)

Rows 4 to 14: 1 sc in each st, ch 1, turn.

Row 15: 1 sc in each st, ch 1, rotate the work 90 degrees clockwise and work 15 sc along the side of the vest, working in the spaces between rows. When you reach the top edge, crochet 20 slst in the remaining loops of the foundation chain. Then ch 1, rotate the piece 90 degrees clockwise again and work 15 sc along the other side of the vest, working in the spaces between rows *(see Techniques: Edging of Flat Pieces)*.

Fasten off and weave in ends.

AVIATOR HAT

Round 1: Using **light brown** for the hat, 6 sc in a magic ring. (6 sts)

Round 2: 2 sc in each st. (12 sts)

Round 3: *1 sc, 2 sc in the next st, rep from * to end. (18 sts)

Round 4: *2 sc, 2 sc in the next st, rep from * to end. (24 sts)

Round 5: *3 sc, 2 sc in the next st, rep from * to end. (30 sts)

Round 6: *4 sc, 2 sc in the next st, rep from * to end. (36 sts)

Round 7: *5 sc, 2 sc in the next st, rep from * to end. (42 sts)

Round 8: *13 sc, 2 sc in the next st, rep from * to end. (45 sts)

Rounds 9 to 15: 1 sc in each st.

Round 16: 3 sc, 20 sc FLO, 22 sc.

From now on we will be crocheting in rows, to make the first ear flap.

Rows 17 and 18: 8 sc, ch 1, turn.

Row 19: sc2tog, 4 sc, sc2tog, ch 1, turn. (6 sts)

Row 20: 1 sc in each st, ch 1, turn.

Row 21: sc2tog, 2 sc, sc2tog, ch 1, turn. (4 sts)

Row 22: 1 sc in each st, ch 1, turn.

Row 23: (sc2tog) twice, ch 1, turn. (2 sts)

Row 24: 1 sc in each st.

Fasten off and weave in ends.

Count 20 sts around from the start of the first ear flap and join in the **light brown** yarn with a slip knot for the second ear flap.

Row 1: 8 sc, ch 1, turn.

Row 2: sc2tog, 4 sc, sc2tog, ch 1, turn. (6 sts)

Row 3: 1 sc in each st, ch 1, turn.

Row 4: sc2tog, 2 sc, sc2tog, ch 1, turn. (4 sts)

Row 5: 1 sc in each st, ch 1, turn.

Row 6: (sc2tog) twice, ch 1, turn. (2 sts)

Row 7: 1 sc in each st.

Do not fasten off. Work one round of sc all around the edge of the hat and both ear flaps.

Fasten off and weave in ends.

HAIR

Using **dark brown** for the hair, attach with a slip knot in the first remaining back loop of round 16.

Row 1: 1 slst in first back loop, ch 11, 1 sc in the second ch from hook, 1 sc in each ch to end (10 sc), *1 slst in next back loop, ch 11, 1 sc in the second ch from hook, 1 sc in each ch to end (10 sc), rep from * to last st, 1 slst in last st. (19 hair curls)

Fasten off, and weave in ends.

GOGGLES

First you will crochet the lenses and then you'll join them to form the goggles.

LENS 1

Round 1: Using **white** for the lens, 6 sc in a magic ring. (6 sts)

Round 2: 2 sc in each st. (12 sts)

Fasten off, and weave in ends. Set aside.

LENS 2

Round 1: Using **white** for the lens, 6 sc in a magic ring. (6 sts)

Round 2: 2 sc in each st. (12 sts)

Round 3: Change to **dark brown** for the googles, and working through BLO for each st, *1 sc, 2 sc in the next st, rep from * to end. (18 sts). Still with lens 2 on your hook, ch 4 and join to lens 1 as follows: working through BLO, *1 sc, 2 sc in the next st, rep from * to end of lens 1 (18 sc), 1 sc in each ch of ch-4-loop, 1 slst in first st of the round to finish.

Fasten off, and weave in ends.

STRAP

Row 1: Using **dark brown**, ch 51, 1 sc in the second ch from hook, 1sc in each ch to end. (50 sts).

Fasten off, leaving a long tail to sew to goggles.

ASSEMBLY

Sew the aviator hat to Amelia's head. Embroider some hair locks on her forehead.

Sew the arms to the sides of the body *(see Techniques: Sewing the Arms)*.

Place arms through vest armholes. Fix vest in place with a few stitches.

Sew the goggles to the aviator hat, in line with Amelia's eyes. Then surround the hat with the strap and sew it to the sides of the goggles.

Weave in all ends inside the doll.

"Never do things others can do and will do, if there are things others cannot do or will not do."

MATERIALS

2.5mm (C/2) crochet hook

100% 8-ply cotton;
colours used: skin colour,
black, light grey, light
turquoise, white, pink

Yarn needle

8mm (⅓in) safety eyes

Stitch marker

Fibrefill stuffing

FINISHED SIZE

20cm (7¾in) tall

QUEEN
ELIZABETH II

Why Her Majesty the Queen? Because she is the longest reigning
monarch in British history, which means that she has dedicated her
entire life in service to her country, putting herself and her interests
always second. She is an example of dedication and sense of duty; of
hard work and determination; of resilience and adaptability. She has
been a privileged witness of all major events of the 20th century and
has successfully rendered her reign more modern, open and sensitive
to a changing public, while maintaining the traditions associated with
the Crown. For me, she is the living symbol of British culture.

LEG 1

Round 1: Using **black** for the shoes, 6 sc in a magic ring. (6 sts)

Round 2: 2 sc in each st. (12 sts)

Rounds 3 and 4: 1 sc in each st.

Round 5: Change to **skin** colour, 1 sc BLO in each st.

Rounds 6 to 8: 1 sc in each st.

Round 9: Change to **white** for the underwear, 1 sc BLO in each st. Fasten off. Set aside.

LEG 2

Work as for Leg 1, but do not fasten off yarn at the end. We will continue with the body.

BODY

Round 10: Still with leg 2 on your hook, ch 3 and join to leg 1 with a sc *(see Techniques: Joining Legs)*, place a stitch marker here for new beg of round, work 11 sc all along leg 1, 1 sc into each ch of 3-ch-loop, 12 sc all along leg 2 and 1 sc into other side of each ch of 3-ch-loop. (30 sts)

Round 11: *4 sc, 2 sc in the next st, rep from * to end. (36 sts)

Rounds 12 to 16: 1 sc in each st.

Round 17: *4 sc, sc2tog, rep from * to end. (30 sts)

Rounds 18 to 20: 1 sc in each st. Stuff the legs firmly at this point.

Round 21: *3 sc, sc2tog, rep from * to end. (24 sts)

Rounds 22 and 23: 1 sc in each st.

Round 24: *2 sc, sc2tog, rep from * to end. (18 sts)
Stuff the body firmly at this point.

Rounds 25 to 27: 1 sc in each st.

Round 28: *1 sc, sc2tog, rep from * to end. (12 sts)

Round 29: Change to **light turquoise** for the coat, 1 sc in each st.

Round 30: Change to **black** for the collar, 1 sc BLO in each st.

Round 31: Change to **skin** colour, 1 sc BLO in each st.
Do not fasten off yarn. We will continue with the head.

HEAD

Round 32: 2 sc in each st. (24 sts)

Round 33: *3 sc, 2 sc in the next st, rep from * to end. (30 sts)
Stuff the neck area firmly at this point.

Round 34: *4 sc, 2 sc in the next st, rep from * to end. (36 sts)

Round 35: *5 sc, 2 sc in the next st, rep from * to end. (42 sts)

Round 36: 1 sc in each st.

Round 37: 24 sc, 1 bobble st for the nose *(see Stitches: Bobble st)*, 1 sc in each st to end. Be sure to align the nose with the middle of the legs and adjust the positioning if necessary.

We will now start crocheting the coat, as it will be easier to do so without the finished head. Place a stitch marker in the loop on your hook to secure it and cut the yarn.

"I declare before you all that my whole life, whether it be long or short, shall be devoted to your service and the service of our great imperial family to which we all belong."

COAT

Turn the body upside down and join **light turquoise** yarn in one of the front loops of round 30, at the back of the neck.

Round 1: *1 sc, 2 sc in the next st, rep from * to end. (18 sts)

Rounds 2 and 3: 1 sc in each st.

Round 4: *2 sc, 2 sc in the next st, rep from * to end. (24 sts)

Rounds 5 and 6: 1 sc in each st.

Round 7: *3 sc, 2 sc in the next st, rep from * to end. (30 sts)

Rounds 8 to 11: 1 sc in each st.

Round 12: *4 sc, 2 sc in the next st, rep from * to end. (36 sts)

Rounds 13 to 15: 1 sc in each st.

Round 16: *5 sc, 2 sc in the next st, rep from * to end. (42 sts)

Rounds 17 to 19: 1 sc in each st.

Round 20: *6 sc, 2 sc in the next st, rep from * to end. (48 sts)

Rounds 21 to 23: 1 sc in each st.

Fasten off and weave in ends.

COLLAR

Turn the body upside down again and join **black** yarn in one of the front loops of round 31, at the back of the neck.

Round 1: 1 sc FLO in each st. (12 sts)

Round 2: 4 sc, (1 hdc and 1 dc) in next st, 3 dc in next st, 1 slst, (1 slst, ch 2, 2 dc in the base of the ch-2) in next st, (1 dc, 1 hdc) in next st, 3 sc.

Fasten off and weave in ends.

Using **black** yarn, embroider three small knots to resemble buttons to top of coat, centrally and in a vertical line.

We will now continue with the head. Rejoin the **skin** colour yarn to where you stopped working the head.

Rounds 38 to 46: 1 sc in each st.

Round 47: *5 sc, sc2tog, rep from * to end. (36 sts)

Start stuffing the head at this point.

Round 48: *4 sc, sc2tog, rep from * to end. (30 sts)

Place safety eyes one round above the nose, with 8 sts between them, embroider cheeks with **pink** yarn.

Round 49: *3 sc, sc2tog, rep from * to end. (24 sts)

Round 50: *2 sc, sc2tog, rep from * to end. (18 sts)

Stuff firmly.

Round 51: *1 sc, sc2tog, rep from * to end. (12 sts)

Round 52: (sc2tog) 6 times. (6 sts)

Fasten off and weave in ends.

TIP

Her Majesty is usually seen wearing gloves matching her outfit, so you can replace the skin colour part of the arms for white (or the colour of your choice) and your Queen will have gloves!

ARMS (MAKE TWO)

Round 1: Using **skin** colour, ch 2, 4 sc in the second ch from hook. (4 sts)

Round 2: 2 sc in each st. (8 sts)

Rounds 3 to 5: 1 sc in each st.

Round 6: Change to **black** yarn, 1 sc BLO in each st.

Round 7: 1 sc in each st.

Round 8: Change to **light turquoise** yarn, 1 sc BLO in each st.

Rounds 9 to 17: 1 sc in each st.

There is no need to stuff the arms.

Round 18: Press the opening with your fingers, aligning 4 sts side by side and sc both sides together by working 1 into each pair of sts *(see Techniques: Closing the Arms)*.

Fasten off, leaving a long tail to sew to the body.

HAIR

Round 1: Using **light grey** for the hair, 6 sc in a magic ring. (6 sts)

Round 2: 2 sc in each st. (12 sts)

Round 3: *1 sc, 2 sc in the next st, rep from * to end. (18 sts)

Round 4: *2 sc, 2 sc in the next st, rep from * to end. (24 sts)

Round 5: *3 sc, 2 sc in the next st, rep from * to end. (30 sts)

Round 6: *4 sc, 2 sc in the next st, rep from * to end. (36 sts)

Round 7: *5 sc, 2 sc in the next st, rep from * to end. (42 sts)

Round 8: *13 sc, 2 sc in the next st, rep from * to end. (45 sts)

Rounds 9 to 16: 1 sc in each st.

Round 17: 1 slst, 6 sc, 1 hdc, 10 dc, 1 hdc, 6 sc, *1 slst in next st, ch 9, 1 sc in the second ch from hook, 1 sc in each st along ch, rep from * to last st, 1 slst. (19 hair curls)

Fasten off, leaving a long tail to sew to the head.

HAT

Round 1: Using **light turquoise** for the hat, 6 sc in a magic ring. (6 sts)

Round 2: 2 sc in each st. (12 sts)

Round 3: 2 sc in each st. (24 sts)

Round 4: *3 sc, 2 sc in the next st, rep from * to end. (30 sts)

Round 5: *4 sc, 2 sc in the next st, rep from * to end. (36 sts)

Round 6: *5 sc, 2 sc in the next st, rep from * to end. (42 sts)

Round 7: *2 sc, 2 sc in the next st, rep from * to end. (56 sts)

Round 8: 1 sc in each st.

Round 9: 1 sc BLO in each st.

Round 10: *6 sc, sc2tog, rep from * to end. (49 sts)

Rounds 11 to 15: 1 sc in each st.

Round 16: Change to **black** yarn, 1 sc in each st.

Round 17: 1 sc in each st.

Round 18: Change to **light turquoise** yarn, working ALL sts in BLO, 1 sc, *1 sc, 2 sc in the next st, rep from * to end. (73 sts)

Round 19: 1 sc in each st.

Round 20: 1 sc, *2 sc, 2 sc in the next st, rep from * to end. (97 sts)

Round 21: 1 sc in each st.

Fasten off and weave in ends.

FLOWERS (MAKE ONE IN WHITE, ONE IN PINK)

For detailed photographs of how to work the flowers see
Techniques: Flowers.

Round 1: Using chosen colour, 5 sc in a magic ring. (5 sts)

Round 2: *1 slst in the next st, ch 2, yarn over, insert hook into the same
st, yarn over and pull yarn through the st. Yarn over, pull yarn through
first 2 loops on hook. Yarn over, insert hook into the same st, yarn over
and pull yarn through the st. Yarn over, pull yarn through first 2 loops on
hook. Yarn over, pull yarn through the 3 remaining loops on hook, ch 2, 1
slst in same st to complete first petal. Repeat from * a further 4 times to
make 5 petals; finish with 1 slst in the next st. (5 petals)

Fasten off, leaving a long tail to sew to the hat.

PURSE

Round 1: Using **black** yarn, ch 7, 2 sc in the second ch from hook, 1 sc
in each of next 4 ch, 4 sc in last ch, turn and work on the other side of the
foundation chain, 1 sc in each of next 4 ch, 2 sc in last ch. (16 sts)

Rounds 2 to 6: 1 sc in each st.

Fasten off and weave in ends.

PURSE STRAP

Using **black** yarn and leaving a long tail at the beginning, ch 15. Fasten
off leaving a long tail.

Using a yarn needle, sew the strap to the purse using both tails.

ASSEMBLY

Sew the hair to the head *(see Techniques: Sewing the Hair)*.

Sew the arms to the sides of the body *(see Techniques: Sewing
the Arms)*.

Sew the flowers to the hat, slightly to the left.

Place the **black** purse on the arm and sew the arm in position to hold the
purse with a few stitches.

Weave in all ends inside the doll.

MATERIALS

FOR JANE

2.5mm (C/2) crochet hook

100% 8-ply cotton; colours used: skin colour, light blue, beige, light brown, light grey, small amount of pink, yellow (optional for bag)

Yarn needle

8mm (⅓in) safety eyes

Stitch marker

Fibrefill stuffing

FOR FLINT, JANE'S CHIMPANZEE

2mm (B/1) crochet hook

100% 4-ply cotton; colours used: beige, dark brown

6mm (¼in) safety eyes for the chimpanzee

FINISHED SIZE

JANE
20cm (7¾in) tall

FLINT
12cm (4¾in) tall

Please note that Flint, the little chimpanzee, is crocheted with a smaller hook and thinner yarn.

JANE GOODALL

Why Jane? Because as the world's leading primatologist, she has redefined the way to study animals in their natural habitats. Ever curious and brave, she spent many years in isolation with wild chimpanzees, immersing herself in their lives to observe them in a completely untraditional and non-threatening way. Her breakthrough research answered many important questions about human evolution. Today, through her foundation, she advocates for ecological preservation, touring the world to teach about conservation, and has become a global animal rights activist, fighting for the ethical treatment of all creatures.

LEG 1

Round 1: Using **light brown** for the boots, 6 sc in a magic ring. (6 sts)

Round 2: 2 sc in each st. (12 sts)

Rounds 3 to 6: 1 sc in each st.

Round 7: Change to **beige** for the pants, 1 sc BLO in each st.

Rounds 8 and 9: 1 sc in each st.

Fasten off. Set aside.

LEG 2

Work as for Leg 1, but do not fasten off yarn at the end. We will continue with the body.

BODY

Round 10: Still with leg 2 on your hook, ch 3 and join to leg 1 with a sc *(see Techniques: Joining Legs)*, place a stitch marker here for new beg of round, work 11 sc all along leg 1, 1 sc into each ch of 3-ch-loop, 12 sc all along leg 2 and 1 sc into other side of each ch of 3-ch-loop. (30 sts)

Round 11: *4 sc, 2 sc in the next st, rep from * to end. (36 sts)

Rounds 12 to 15: 1 sc in each st.

Round 16: Change to **light brown** for the belt, 1 sc BLO in each st.

Round 17: *4 sc, sc2tog, rep from * to end. (30 sts)

Round 18: Change to **light blue** for the shirt, 1 sc BLO in each st.

Rounds 19 and 20: 1 sc in each st.

Stuff the legs firmly at this point.

Round 21: *3 sc, sc2tog, rep from * to end. (24 sts)

Rounds 22 and 23: 1 sc in each st.

Round 24: *2 sc, sc2tog, rep from * to end. (18 sts)

Stuff the body firmly at this point.

Rounds 25 and 26: 1 sc in each st.

Round 27: *1 sc, sc2tog, rep from * to end. (12 sts)

Round 28: 1 sc in each st.

Round 29: 7 sc, change to **skin** colour, 1 sc, change back to **light blue**, 4 sc.

Round 30: 6 sc, change to **skin** colour, 3 sc, change back to **light blue**, 3 sc.

Round 31: 5 sc, change to **skin** colour, 5 sc, change back to **light blue**, 2 sc.

You should have a **skin** colour triangle at the front centre of the doll. Do not fasten off yarn. We will continue with the head.

"Every individual matters. Every individual has a role to play. Every individual makes a difference."

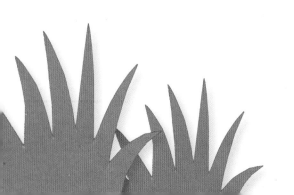

HEAD

Round 32: Change to **skin** colour, 2 sc BLO in each of the first 5 sts (those in **light blue**), 2 sc through both loops in each of the following 5 sts (those in **skin** colour), 2 sc BLO in each of last 2 sts (those in **light blue**). (24 sts)

Round 33: *3 sc, 2 sc in the next st, rep from * to end. (30 sts) Stuff the neck area firmly at this point.

Round 34: *4 sc, 2 sc in the next st, rep from * to end. (36 sts)

Round 35: *5 sc, 2 sc in the next st, rep from * to end. (42 sts)

Round 36: 1 sc in each st.

Round 37: 26 sc, 1 bobble st for the nose *(see Stitches: Bobble st)*, 1 sc in each st to end. Be sure to align the nose with the middle of the legs, and the **skin** colour triangle at the neck, and adjust the positioning if necessary.

We will take a break here from the head to work the collar of Jane's shirt. Place a stitch marker in the loop on your hook to secure.

For detailed photographs of how to work a collar see *Techniques: Creating the V Collar*.

Join the **light blue** yarn 2 rounds below the tip of the **skin** triangle. Work in the spaces between stitches and crochet 2 surface sc up until you reach the bottom tip of the triangle.

Now follow the diagonal of the triangle, working the right side first. Crochet 1 surface sc in between each round, inserting the hook in the spaces between rounds, until you reach the round where the **light blue** front loops are showing.

Now crochet 2 sc in each front loop of the shirt bordering Jane's neck, until you reach the edge of the triangle on the other side (14 sts). Work 5 surface sc in between rounds following the diagonal of the triangle to the starting stitch, work 1 slst in the starting stitch.

Fasten off and weave in ends.

We will now continue with the head. Rejoin the **skin** colour yarn to where you stopped working the head.

Rounds 38 to 46: 1 sc in each st.

Round 47: *5 sc, sc2tog, rep from * to end. (36 sts)

Start stuffing the head at this point.

Round 48: *4 sc, sc2tog, rep from * to end. (30 sts)

Place safety eyes one round above the nose, with 8 sts between them, embroider cheeks with **pink** yarn.

Round 49: *3 sc, sc2tog, rep from * to end. (24 sts)

Round 50: *2 sc, sc2tog, rep from * to end. (18 sts)

Stuff firmly.

Round 51: *1 sc, sc2tog, rep from * to end. (12 sts)

Round 52: (sc2tog) 6 times. (6 sts)

Fasten off and weave in ends.

TIP

If you don't want to do Jane's collar with surface single crochet, just embroider two diagonal lines using the colour of her shirt, to mark the edges of the skin triangle showing on her neck.

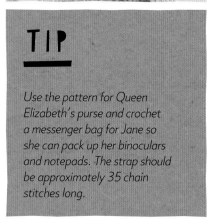

TIP

Use the pattern for Queen Elizabeth's purse and crochet a messenger bag for Jane so she can pack up her binoculars and notepads. The strap should be approximately 35 chain stitches long.

ARMS (MAKE TWO)

Round 1: Using **skin** colour, ch 2, 4 sc in the second ch from hook. (4 sts)

Round 2: 2 sc in each st. (8 sts)

Rounds 3 to 8: 1 sc in each st.

Round 9: Change to **light blue** yarn, 1 sc BLO in each st.

Rounds 10 to 17: 1 sc in each st.

There is no need to stuff the arms.

Round 18: Press the opening with your fingers, aligning 4 sts side by side and sc both sides together by working 1 sc into each pair of sts *(see Techniques: Closing the Arms)*.

Fasten off, leaving a long tail to sew to the body.

HAIR

Round 1: Using **light grey** for the hair, 6 sc in a magic ring. (6 sts)

Round 2: 2 sc in each st. (12 sts)

Round 3: *1 sc, 2 sc in the next st, rep from * to end. (18 sts)

Round 4: *2 sc, 2 sc in the next st, rep from * to end. (24 sts)

Round 5: *3 sc, 2 sc in the next st, rep from * to end. (30 sts)

Round 6: *4 sc, 2 sc in the next st, rep from * to end. (36 sts)

Round 7: *5 sc, 2 sc in the next st, rep from * to end. (42 sts)

Round 8: *13 sc, 2 sc in the next st, rep from * to end. (45 sts)

Rounds 9 to 15: 1 sc in each st.

Round 16: 1 slst, *1 sc, 1 hdc, 10 dc, 1 hdc, 1 sc, 1 slst, rep from * once more, leave the rest of the stitches unworked.

Fasten off, leaving a long tail to sew to the head.

PONYTAIL LOCKS (MAKE FOUR)

Row 1: Using **light grey** yarn, ch 21, 1 sc in the second ch from hook, 1 sc in each ch to end. (20 sts)

Fasten off, leaving a long tail to sew to the head.

ASSEMBLY

Sew the hair to Jane's head *(see Techniques: Sewing the Hair)*.

Sew the four locks of hair to the back of Jane's hair, above her neck, to create her iconic ponytail. Wrap the ponytail with a bit of **light blue** yarn.

Sew the arms to the sides of the body *(see Techniques: Sewing the Arms)*.

Weave in all ends inside the doll.

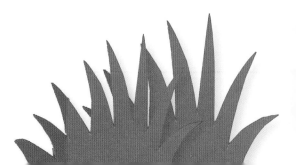

FLINT, JANE'S CHIMPANZEE

BODY

Round 1: Using **dark brown** for the fur, 6 sc in a magic ring. (6 sts)

Round 2: 2 sc in each st. (12 sts)

Round 3: *1 sc, 2 sc in the next st, rep from * to end. (18 sts)

Round 4: *2 sc, 2 sc in the next st, rep from * to end. (24 sts)

Rounds 5 to 9: 1 sc in each st.

Round 10: *2 sc, sc2tog, rep from * to end. (18 sts)

Rounds 11 to 13: 1 sc in each st.

Stuff firmly at this point.

Round 14: *1 sc, sc2tog, rep from * to end. (12 sts)

Rounds 15 to 18: 1 sc in each st.

We will now continue with the head.

HEAD

Round 19: Change to **skin** colour, 2 sc BLO in each st. (24 sts)

Round 20: *1 sc, 2 sc in the next st, rep from * to end. (36 sts)

Stuff the neck area firmly at this point.

Rounds 21 to 31: 1 sc in each st.

Place safety eyes between rounds 24 and 25, with 7 sts between them, embroider mouth with **dark brown** yarn.

Round 32: *4 sc, sc2tog, rep from * to end. (30 sts)

Round 33: *3 sc, sc2tog, rep from * to end. (24 sts)

Round 34: *2 sc, sc2tog, rep from * to end. (18 sts)

Stuff firmly.

Round 35: *1 sc, sc2tog, rep from * to end. (12 sts)

Round 36: (sc2tog) 6 times. (6 sts)

Fasten off and weave in ends.

HEAD FUR

Round 1: Using **dark brown** for the fur, 6 sc in a magic ring. (6 sts)

Round 2: 2 sc in each st. (12 sts)

Round 3: *1 sc, 2 sc in the next st, rep from * to end. (18 sts)

Round 4: *2 sc, 2 sc in the next st, rep from * to end. (24 sts)

Round 5: *3 sc, 2 sc in the next st, rep from * to end. (30 sts)

Round 6: *4 sc, 2 sc in the next st, rep from * to end. (36 sts)

Round 7: *11 sc, 2 sc in the next st, rep from * to end. (39 sts)

Rounds 8 to 14: 1 sc in each st.

Round 15: 18 sc, 1 hdc, (1 hdc, 1 picot *(see Stitches: Picot st)*, 1 hdc) in next st, 1 hdc, 18 sc.

Fasten off, leaving a long tail to sew to the head.

EARS (MAKE TWO)

Round 1: Using **skin** colour, 6 sc in a magic ring. (6 sts)

Round 2: 2 sc in each st. (12 sts)

Rounds 3 and 4: 1 sc in each st.

Round 5: (sc2tog) 6 times. (6 sts)

Fasten off, flatten with your fingers and secure with a few stitches using a yarn needle. Leave a long tail at one side, to sew later to the head.

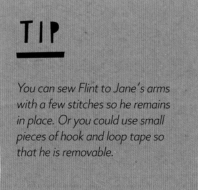

TIP

You can sew Flint to Jane's arms with a few stitches so he remains in place. Or you could use small pieces of hook and loop tape so that he is removable.

ARMS (MAKE TWO)

Round 1: Using **skin** colour, ch 2, 4 sc in the second ch from hook. (4 sts)

Round 2: 2 sc in each st. (8 sts)

Rounds 3 to 5: 1 sc in each st.

Round 6: Change to **dark brown** yarn, 1 sc BLO in each st.

There is no need to stuff the arms.

Rounds 7 to 15: 1 sc in each st.

Round 16: Press the opening with your fingers, aligning 4 sts side by side and sc both sides together by working 1 sc into each pair of sts *(see Techniques: Closing the Arms).*

Fasten off, leaving a long tail to sew to the body.

LEGS (MAKE TWO)

Round 1: Using **skin** colour, 5 sc in a magic ring. (5 sts)

Round 2: 2 sc in each st. (10 sts)

Rounds 3 to 5: 1 sc in each st.

Round 6: Change to **dark brown** yarn, 1 sc BLO in each st.

There is no need to stuff the legs.

Rounds 7 to 15: 1 sc in each st.

Round 16: Press the opening with your fingers, aligning 5 sts side by side and sc both sides together by working 1 sc into each pair of sts *(see Techniques: Closing the Arms).*

Fasten off, leaving a long tail to sew to the body.

MONKEY TAIL

Round 1: Using **dark brown** yarn, leaving a long initial tail, ch 21, 1 sc in the second ch from the hook, 1 sc in each ch to end. (20 sts)

Fasten off, leaving a long tail to sew to the body.

ASSEMBLY

Sew the fur cap to the monkey's head. Sew the ears to the sides of the head.

Sew the legs to the base of the body *(see Techniques: Sewing the Arms).*

Sew the arms to the sides of the body *(see Techniques: Sewing the Arms).*

Sew the tail to the back of the body. Weave in all ends inside the doll.

MATERIALS

2.5mm (C/2)
crochet hook

100% 8-ply cotton;
colours used: skin
colour, black, brown,
light grey or silver,
small amount of pink

Yarn needle

8mm (⅓in) safety eyes

Stitch marker

Fibrefill stuffing

FINISHED SIZE

20cm (7¾in) tall

AUDREY HEPBURN

Why Audrey? Because she is one of Hollywood's greatest style icons and her movies have become cinematic classics: "Roman Holiday", "Sabrina", "Funny Face", "My Fair Lady" and "Breakfast at Tiffany's". But with all her fame and success, she never forgot her suffering as a child during World War II. She slowly left her acting career to devote her time to children in need. As a humanitarian, she became a Goodwill Ambassador for UNICEF, and dedicated her final years to visiting sick children around the world, using her spotlight to shine a light on child famine.

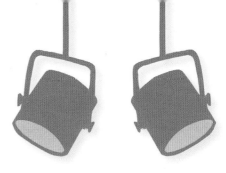

LEG 1

Round 1: Using **skin** colour, 6 sc in a magic ring. (6 sts)

Round 2: 2 sc in each st. (12 sts)

Rounds 3 to 8: 1 sc in each st.

Round 9: Change to **black** for the underwear, 1 sc BLO in each st.

Fasten off. Set aside.

Note: *Hubert de Givenchy designed the iconic dress Audrey used in the opening scene of "Breakfast at Tiffany's". Although it won't show, such a dress deserves black underwear! Do not use white!*

LEG 2

Work as for Leg 1, but do not fasten off yarn at the end. We will continue with the body.

BODY

Round 10: Still with leg 2 on your hook, ch 3 and join to leg 1 with a sc *(see Techniques: Joining Legs)*, place a stitch marker here for new beg of round, work 11 sc all along leg 1, 1 sc into each ch of 3-ch-loop, 12 sc all along leg 2 and 1 sc into other side of each ch of 3-ch-loop. (30 sts)

Round 11: *4 sc, 2 sc in the next st, rep from * to end. (36 sts)

Rounds 12 to 16: 1 sc in each st.

Round 17: 1 sc BLO in each st.

Stuff the legs firmly at this point.

Round 18: *4 sc, sc2tog, rep from * to end. (30 sts)

Rounds 19 and 20: 1 sc in each st.

Round 21: *3 sc, sc2tog, rep from * to end. (24 sts)

Rounds 22 and 23: 1 sc in each st.

Round 24: *2 sc, sc2tog, rep from * to end. (18 sts)

Stuff the body firmly at this point.

Rounds 25 and 26: 1 sc in each st.

Round 27: *1 sc, sc2tog, rep from * to end. (12 sts)

Round 28: Change to **skin** colour, 1 sc BLO in each st.

Rounds 29 to 31: 1 sc in each st.

Do not fasten off yarn. We will continue with the head.

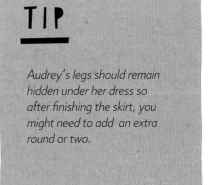

TIP

Audrey's legs should remain hidden under her dress so after finishing the skirt, you might need to add an extra round or two.

HEAD

Round 32: 2 sc in each st. (24 sts)

Round 33: *3 sc, 2 sc in the next st, rep from * to end. (30 sts)

Stuff the neck area firmly at this point.

Round 34: *4 sc, 2 sc in the next st, rep from * to end. (36 sts)

Round 35: *5 sc, 2 sc in the next st, rep from * to end. (42 sts)

Round 36: 1 sc in each st.

Round 37: 26 sc, 1 bobble st for the nose *(see Stitches: Bobble st)*, 1 sc in each st to end. Be sure to align the nose with the middle of the legs and adjust the positioning if necessary.

Rounds 38 to 46: 1 sc in each st.

Round 47: *5 sc, sc2tog, rep from * to end. (36 sts)

Start stuffing the head at this point.

Round 48: *4 sc, sc2tog, rep from * to end. (30 sts)

Place safety eyes one round above the nose, with 8 sts between them, embroider cheeks with **pink** yarn.

Round 49: *3 sc, sc2tog, rep from * to end. (24 sts)

Round 50: *2 sc, sc2tog, rep from * to end. (18 sts)

Stuff firmly.

Round 51: *1 sc, sc2tog, rep from * to end. (12 sts)

Round 52: (sc2tog) 6 times. (6 sts)

Fasten off and weave in ends.

SKIRT OF AUDREY'S GIVENCHY DRESS

Turn the body upside down and join **black** yarn in one of the front loops of round 17, at the back of the body.

Round 1: 1 sc FLO in each st of round 17. (36 sts)

Rounds 2 and 3: 1 sc in each st.

Round 4: *5 sc, 2 sc in the next st, rep from * to end. (42 sts)

Rounds 5 to 11: 1 sc in each st.

Round 12: *5 sc, sc2tog, rep from * to end. (36 sts)

Rounds 13 to 16: 1 sc in each st.

Round 17: 1 slst in each st.

Fasten off and weave in ends.

ARMS (MAKE TWO)

Round 1: Using **black** for Audrey's gloves, ch 2, 4 sc in the second ch from hook. (4 sts)

Round 2: 2 sc in each st. (8 sts)

Rounds 3 to 11: 1 sc in each st.

Round 12: Change to **skin** colour, 1 sc BLO in each st.

Rounds 13 to 17: 1 sc in each st.

There is no need to stuff the arms.

Round 18: Press the opening with your fingers, aligning 4 sts side by side and sc both sides together by working 1 sc into each pair of sts *(see Techniques: Closing the Arms)*.

Fasten off, leaving a long tail to sew to the body.

HAIR

Round 1: Using **brown** for the hair, 6 sc in a magic ring. (6 sts)

Round 2: 2 sc in each st. (12 sts)

Round 3: *1 sc, 2 sc in the next st, rep from * to end. (18 sts)

Round 4: *2 sc, 2 sc in the next st, rep from * to end. (24 sts)

Round 5: *3 sc, 2 sc in the next st, rep from * to end. (30 sts)

Round 6: *4 sc, 2 sc in the next st, rep from * to end. (36 sts)

Round 7: *5 sc, 2 sc in the next st, rep from * to end. (42 sts)

Round 8: *13 sc, 2 sc in the next st, rep from * to end. (45 sts)

Rounds 9 to 15: 1 sc in each st.

Round 16: 1 slst, 1 sc, 1 hdc, 8 dc, 1 hdc, 1 sc, 2 slst, *ch 6, 1 sc in the second ch from hook, 1 sc in each st along ch (5 sts), 2 slst, rep from * twice, 1 sc, 1 hdc, 8 dc, 1 hdc, 1 sc, 1 slst. Leave the rest of the stitches in the round unworked.

Fasten off, leaving a long tail to sew to the head.

HAIRBUN

Round 1: Using **brown**, 6 sc in a magic ring. (6 sts)

Round 2: 2 sc in each st. (12 sts)

Round 3: *1 sc, 2 sc in the next st, rep from * to end. (18 sts)

Round 4: *2 sc, 2 sc in the next st, rep from * to end. (24 sts)

Round 5: *3 sc, 2 sc in the next st, rep from * to end. (30 sts)

Rounds 6 to 8: 1 sc in each st.

Round 9: *3 sc, sc2tog, rep from * to end. (24 sts)

Fasten off, leaving a long tail to sew to the head.

"Nothing is impossible, the word itself says 'I'm possible'!"

TIARA

Row 1: Using **light grey** or **silver** yarn, ch 6, 1 slst in second ch from hook, 1 sc, (1 hdc, 1 dc, 1 hdc) all in the same stitch, 1 sc, 1 slst. (7 sts)

Fasten off, leaving a long tail to sew to the head.

NECKLACE

Using **light grey** or **silver** yarn and leaving a long tail at the beginning, ch 24.

Fasten off leaving a long tail.

ASSEMBLY

Sew the hair to the head *(see Techniques: Sewing the Hair)*.

Sew the arms to the sides of the body *(see Techniques: Sewing the Arms)*.

Stuff and sew the hairbun to Audrey's hair, right on top.

Sew the tiara in between the hair and the hairbun.

Knot the necklace around Audrey's neck.

Weave in all ends inside the doll.

TIP

Can't find silver yarn and you really want the tiara and necklace to sparkle? Then use silver embroidery floss and grab it together with the silver yarn when crocheting!

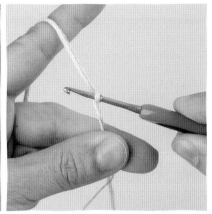

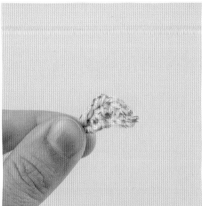

TIP

Consider making Audrey's necklace with beads or tiny plastic pearls. The necklace she used in the movie "Breakfast at Tiffany's" has in fact a huge brooch in the middle and several strands of pearls.

MATERIALS

2.5mm (C/2)
crochet hook

100% 8-ply cotton;
colours used: skin
colour, black, white,
small amount of pink

Yarn needle

8mm (⅓in) safety eyes

Stitch marker

Fibrefill stuffing

FINISHED SIZE

20cm (7¾in) tall

BILLIE HOLIDAY

Why Billie? Because she is one of the most influential jazz singers of all time and many believe she set the standard for all singers who came afterwards. In spite of her difficult childhood and upbringing, her infinite resilience, plus her very expressive voice range and skill for improvisation, led her to perform with the biggest names in jazz. But no matter how successful and talented she was, in a time of segregation, she was constantly discriminated against whilst touring. Yet she was not intimidated. On the contrary: her concern for the treatment of black people can be found in the lyrics of her hit song "Strange Fruit", which she bravely performed at high personal cost.

LEG 1

Round 1: Using **skin** colour, 6 sc in a magic ring. (6 sts)

Round 2: 2 sc in each st. (12 sts)

Rounds 3 to 8: 1 sc in each st

Round 9: Change to **white** for the underwear, 1 sc BLO in each st.

Fasten off. Set aside.

LEG 2

Work as for Leg 1, but do not fasten off yarn at the end. We will continue with the body.

BODY

Round 10: Still with leg 2 on your hook, ch 3 and join to leg 1 with a sc *(see Techniques: Joining Legs)*, place a stitch marker here for new beg of round, work 11 sc all along leg 1, 1 sc into each ch of 3-ch-loop, 12 sc all along leg 2 and 1 sc into other side of each ch of 3-ch-loop. (30 sts)

Round 11: *4 sc, 2 sc in the next st, rep from * to end. (36 sts)

Rounds 12 to 15: 1 sc in each st.

Round 16: Change to **skin** colour, 1 sc BLO in each st.

Stuff the legs firmly at this point.

Round 17: *4 sc, sc2tog, rep from * to end. (30 sts)

Round 18: Change to **white** yarn, 1 sc BLO in each st.

Round 19: 1 sc BLO in each st.

Round 20: *3 sc, sc2tog, rep from * to end. (24 sts)

Rounds 21 to 23: 1 sc in each st.

Round 24: *2 sc, sc2tog, rep from * to end. (18 sts)

Stuff the body firmly at this point.

Rounds 25 and 26: 1 sc in each st.

Round 27: Change to **skin** colour, 1 sc BLO in each st.

Round 28: *1 sc, sc2tog, rep from * to end. (12 sts)

Rounds 29 to 31: 1 sc in each st.

Do not fasten off yarn. We will continue with the head.

HEAD

Round 32: 2 sc in each st. (24 sts)

Round 33: *3 sc, 2 sc in the next st, rep from * to end. (30 sts)

Stuff the neck area firmly at this point.

Round 34: *4 sc, 2 sc in the next st, rep from * to end. (36 sts)

Round 35: *5 sc, 2 sc in the next st, rep from * to end. (42 sts)

Round 36: 1 sc in each st.

Round 37: 26 sc, 1 bobble st for the nose *(see Stitches: Bobble st)*, 1 sc in each st to end. Be sure to align the nose with the middle of the legs and adjust the positioning if necessary.

Rounds 38 to 46: 1 sc in each st.

Round 47: *5 sc, sc2tog, rep from * to end. (36 sts)

Start stuffing the head at this point.

Round 48: *4 sc, sc2tog, rep from * to end. (30 sts)

Place safety eyes one round above the nose, with 8 sts between them, embroider cheeks with **pink** yarn.

Round 49: *3 sc, sc2tog, rep from * to end. (24 sts)

Round 50: *2 sc, sc2tog, rep from * to end. (18 sts)

Stuff firmly.

Round 51: *1 sc, sc2tog, rep from * to end. (12 sts)

Round 52: (sc2tog) 6 times. (6 sts)

Fasten off and weave in ends.

TIP

Billie's legs should remain hidden under the skirt of her white dress. This means that, after finishing the skirt, you might need to add an extra round or two. If so, simply repeat the instructions for the last round.

SKIRT OF DRESS

Turn the body upside down and join **white** yarn in one of the front loops of round 19, at the back of the body.

Round 1: 1 sc FLO in each st of round 19. (30 sts)

Round 2: *4 sc, 2 sc in the next st, rep from * to end. (36 sts)

Round 3: 1 sc in each st.

Round 4: *5 sc, 2 sc in the next st, rep from * to end. (42 sts)

Rounds 5 to 7: 1 sc in each st.

Round 8: *6 sc, 2 sc in the next st, rep from * to end. (48 sts)

Rounds 9 to 14: 1 sc in each st.

Round 15: *7 sc, 2 sc in the next st, rep from * to end. (54 sts)

Rounds 16 to 19: 1 sc in each st.

Fasten off and weave in ends.

SHOULDER DRAPES (MAKE TWO)

Row 1: Leaving a long initial tail and using **white** yarn, ch 15, 1 sc in the second ch from hook, 1 sc in each ch to end, ch 1, turn. (14 sts)

Row 2: 1 slst, 1 sc, 1 hdc, 8 dc, 1 hdc, 1 sc, 1 slst.

Fasten off, leaving a long tail to sew to the dress. With your yarn needle, thread one of the ends and work a few stitches to slim the edges.

ARMS (MAKE TWO)

Round 1: Using **skin** colour, ch 2, 4 sc in the second ch from hook. (4 sts)

Round 2: 2 sc in each st. (8 sts)

Rounds 3 to 16: 1 sc in each st.

There is no need to stuff the arms.

Round 17: Press the opening with your fingers, aligning 4 sts side by side and sc both sides together by working 1 sc into each pair of sts *(see Techniques: Closing the Arms)*.

Fasten off, leaving a long tail to sew to the body.

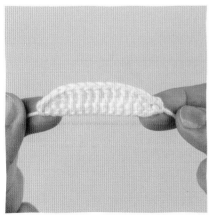

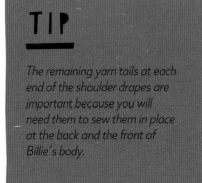

TIP

The remaining yarn tails at each end of the shoulder drapes are important because you will need them to sew them in place at the back and the front of Billie's body.

HAIR

Round 1: Using **black** for the hair, 6 sc in a magic ring. (6 sts)

Round 2: 2 sc in each st. (12 sts)

Round 3: *1 sc, 2 sc in the next st, rep from * to end. (18 sts)

Round 4: *2 sc, 2 sc in the next st, rep from * to end. (24 sts)

Round 5: *3 sc, 2 sc in the next st, rep from * to end. (30 sts)

Round 6: *4 sc, 2 sc in the next st, rep from * to end. (36 sts)

Round 7: *5 sc, 2 sc in the next st, rep from * to end. (42 sts)

Round 8: *13 sc, 2 sc in the next st, rep from * to end. (45 sts)

Rounds 9 to 15: 1 sc in each st.

Round 16: 1 slst, 1 sc, 1 hdc, 8 dc, 1 hdc, 1 sc, 2 slst, *ch 6, 1 sc in the second ch from hook, 1 sc in each st along ch (5 sts), 2 slst, rep from * twice, 1 sc, 1 hdc, 4 dc, 1 hdc, 1 sc, 1 slst. Leave the rest of the stitches in the round unworked.

Fasten off, leaving a long tail to sew to the head.

HAIRBUN

Round 1: Using **black**, 6 sc in a magic ring. (6 sts)

Round 2: 2 sc in each st. (12 sts)

Round 3: *1 sc, 2 sc in the next st, rep from * to end. (18 sts)

Rounds 4 to 7: 1 sc in each st.

Round 8: *1 sc, sc2tog, rep from * to end. (12 sts)

Fasten off, leaving a long tail to sew to the head.

"Southern trees bear a strange fruit,
Blood on the leaves and blood at the root,
Black bodies swinging in the Southern breeze,
Strange fruit hanging from the poplar trees."
"Strange Fruit" written by Lewis Allan,
recorded by Billie Holiday

FLOWERS (MAKE THREE)

For detailed photographs of how to work the flowers see *Techniques: Flowers*.

Round 1: Using **white**, 5 sc in a magic ring. (5 sts)

Round 2: *1 slst in the next st, ch 2 and yarn over, insert the hook into the same st, yarn over and pull yarn through the st. Yarn over, pull yarn through first 2 loops on your hook. Yarn over, insert hook into the same st, yarn over and pull yarn through the st. Yarn over, pull yarn through first 2 loops on your hook. Yarn over, pull yarn through the 3 remaining loops on hook, ch 2, 1 slst in same st to complete first petal. Repeat from * a further 4 times to make 5 petals; finish with 1 slst in the next st. (5 petals)

Fasten off, leaving a long tail to sew to the hair.

ASSEMBLY

Sew the hair to the head *(see Techniques: Sewing the Hair)*. Billie's hair is slightly parted to the right. Secure the loose locks of hair to her forehead with a few stitches.

Stuff and sew the hairbun to Billie's hair, slightly to one side.

Sew the three **white** flowers to one side of the hair, in front of the hairbun.

Sew the arms to the sides of the body *(see Techniques: Sewing the Arms)*.

Sew each shoulder drape from their ends to the chest and back of Billie's body, surrounding the arms.

Weave in all ends inside the doll.

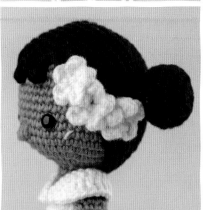

TIP

Billie liked her gardenias to be big! If you have leftovers of thicker white yarn, change your crochet hook and use these instructions to crochet a larger flower!

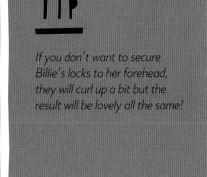
TIP

If you don't want to secure Billie's locks to her forehead, they will curl up a bit but the result will be lovely all the same!

MATERIALS

2.5mm (C/2)
crochet hook

100% 8-ply cotton;
colours used: skin
colour, black, white,
yellow, mint green

Yarn needle

8mm (⅓in) safety eyes

Stitch marker

Fibrefill stuffing

FINISHED SIZE

20cm (7¾in) tall

CLEOPATRA

Why Cleopatra? Because she is still considered one of the most famous female rulers in history. Her life inspired Shakespeare's play "Anthony and Cleopatra" and even actress Elizabeth Taylor incarnated her for the big screen. She was very intelligent and audacious, known for her many charms, shrewdness and high education. And although the Romans considered her the most dangerous seductress, she truly cared about her kingdom, being the only one in her family to learn Egyptian and take an interest in Egyptian culture, which earned her the loyalty of her subjects. In an era of male-domination and internal and external battles, Cleopatra held her country together, proving to be as powerful a leader as any of her male counterparts.

LEG 1

Round 1: Using **skin** colour, 6 sc in a magic ring. (6 sts)

Round 2: 2 sc in each st. (12 sts)

Rounds 3 to 8: 1 sc in each st

Round 9: Change to **white** for the underwear, 1 sc BLO in each st.

Fasten off. Set aside.

LEG 2

Work as for Leg 1, but do not fasten off yarn at the end. We will continue with the body.

BODY

Round 10: Still with leg 2 on your hook, ch 3 and join to leg 1 with a sc *(see Techniques: Joining Legs)*, place a stitch marker here for new beg of round, work 11 sc all along leg 1, 1 sc into each ch of 3-ch-loop, 12 sc all along leg 2 and 1 sc into other side of each ch of 3-ch-loop. (30 sts)

Round 11: *4 sc, 2 sc in the next st, rep from * to end. (36 sts)

Rounds 12 to 16: 1 sc in each st.

Round 17: Change to **yellow** yarn for the belt, 1 sc BLO in each st.

Round 18: *4 sc, sc2tog, rep from * to end. (30 sts)

Round 19: Change back to **white** yarn for the tunic, 1 sc BLO in each st.

Round 20: 1 sc in each st.

Round 21: *3 sc, sc2tog, rep from * to end. (24 sts)

Rounds 22 and 23: 1 sc in each st.

Round 24: *2 sc, sc2tog, rep from * to end. (18 sts)

Stuff the body firmly at this point.

Rounds 25 and 26: 1 sc in each st.

Round 27: *1 sc, sc2tog, rep from * to end. (12 sts)

Rounds 28 and 29: 1 sc in each st.

Round 30: Change to **skin** colour, 1 sc BLO in each st.

Round 31: 1 sc in each st.

Do not fasten off yarn. We will continue with the head.

HEAD

Round 32: 2 sc in each st. (24 sts)

Round 33: *3 sc, 2 sc in the next st, rep from * to end. (30 sts)

Stuff the neck area firmly at this point.

Round 34: *4 sc, 2 sc in the next st, rep from * to end. (36 sts)

Round 35: *5 sc, 2 sc in the next st, rep from * to end. (42 sts)

Round 36: 1 sc in each st.

Round 37: 26 sc, 1 bobble st for the nose *(see Stitches: Bobble st)*, 1 sc in each st to end. Be sure to align the nose with the middle of the legs and adjust the positioning if necessary.

We will now start crocheting Cleopatra's necklace, as it will be easier to do so without the finished head. Place a stitch marker in the loop on your hook to secure it and cut the yarn.

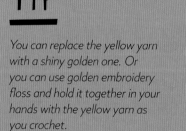

TIP

You can replace the yellow yarn with a shiny golden one. Or you can use golden embroidery floss and hold it together in your hands with the yellow yarn as you crochet.

NECKLACE

Turn the body upside down and join **yellow** yarn in one of the front loops of round 30, at the back of the neck.

Round 1: 1 sc FLO in each st of round 30. (12 sts)

Round 2: Change to **mint green** yarn, *1 sc, 2 sc in the next st, rep from * to end. (18 sts)

Round 3: Change to **yellow** yarn, *1 sc, 2 sc in the next st, rep from * to end. (27 sts)

Round 4: Change to **mint green** yarn, 1 sc in each st.

Round 5: Change to **yellow** yarn, *2 sc, 2 sc in the next st, rep from * to end. (36 sts)

Round 6: Change to **mint green** yarn, 1 sc in each st.

Round 7: 1 slst in each st.

Fasten off and weave in ends.

We will now continue with the head. Rejoin the **skin** colour yarn to where you stopped working the head.

Rounds 38 to 46: 1 sc in each st.

Round 47: *5 sc, sc2tog, rep from * to end. (36 sts)

Start stuffing the head at this point.

Round 48: *4 sc, sc2tog, rep from * to end. (30 sts)

Place safety eyes one round above the nose, with 8 sts between them, embroider eye makeup with **black** yarn.

Round 49: *3 sc, sc2tog, rep from * to end. (24 sts)

Round 50: *2 sc, sc2tog, rep from * to end. (18 sts)

Stuff firmly.

Round 51: *1 sc, sc2tog, rep from * to end. (12 sts)

Round 52: (sc2tog) 6 times. (6 sts)

Fasten off and weave in ends.

SKIRT OF TUNIC

Turn the body upside down and join **white** yarn in one of the front loops of round 19, at the back of the body.

Round 1: 1 sc FLO in each st of round 19. (36 sts)

Round 2: *5 sc, 2 sc in the next st, rep from * to end. (42 sts)

Round 3: *6 sc, 2 sc in the next st, rep from * to end. (48 sts)

Rounds 4 to 8: 1 sc in each st.

Round 9: 1 slst in each st.

Fasten off and weave in ends.

ARMS (MAKE TWO)

Round 1: Using **skin** colour, ch 2, 4 sc in the second ch from hook. (4 sts)

Round 2: 2 sc in each st. (8 sts)

Rounds 3 to 5: 1 sc in each st.

Round 6: Change to **yellow** yarn for the bracelet, 1 sc BLO in each st.

There is no need to stuff the arms.

Rounds 7 to 9: 1 sc in each st.

Round 10: Change back to **skin** colour, 1 sc BLO in each st.

Rounds 11 to 17: 1 sc in each st.

Round 18: Press the opening with your fingers, aligning 4 sts side by side and sc both sides together by working 1 sc into each pair of sts *(see Techniques: Closing the Arms)*.

Fasten off, leaving a long tail to sew to the body.

TIP

Would you like your Cleopatra to have sandals? Then start crocheting her legs with yellow yarn for the first three rounds and remember to change to skin colour on round 4. Then just add straps!

HAIR

Round 1: Using **black** for the hair, 6 sc in a magic ring. (6 sts)

Round 2: 2 sc in each st. (12 sts)

Round 3: *1 sc, 2 sc in the next st, rep from * to end. (18 sts)

Round 4: *2 sc, 2 sc in the next st, rep from * to end. (24 sts)

Round 5: *3 sc, 2 sc in the next st, rep from * to end. (30 sts)

Round 6: *4 sc, 2 sc in the next st, rep from * to end. (36 sts)

Round 7: *5 sc, 2 sc in the next st, rep from * to end. (42 sts)

Round 8: *6 sc, 2 sc in the next st, rep from * to end. (48 sts)

Rounds 9 to 12: 1 sc in each st.

Round 13: Change to **yellow** yarn for the crown, 1 sc BLO in each st.

Round 14: 1 sc in each st.

Round 15: Change back to **black** yarn, 1 sc BLO in each st.

Round 16: 1 sc in the first 11 sts, ch 1, turn, leaving the rest of the stitches unworked. (11 sts)

We will now stop crocheting in rounds and start crocheting in rows.

Row 17: 22 sc, ch 1, turn. (22 sts)

Rows 18 to 24: 1 sc in each st, ch 1, turn.

Row 25: 1 sc in each st, ch 1, rotate the work 90 degrees clockwise and work 8 sc along the side of the bob, working in the spaces between rows.

When you reach the forehead, crochet 23 sc along the edge of the hair piece.

Then ch 1 and work 8 sc along the other side of the bob, working in the spaces between rows.

Fasten off and weave in ends.

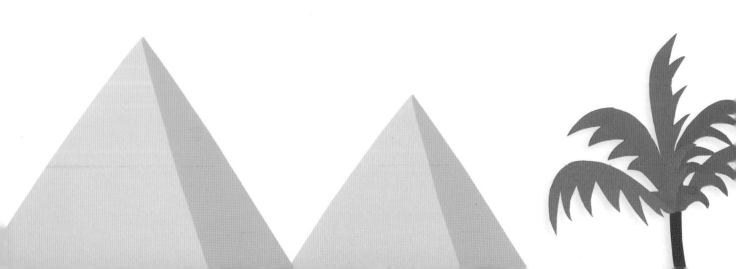

SNAKE FOR THE CROWN

Round 1: Using **yellow** yarn, ch 2, 4 sc in the second ch from hook. (4 sts)

Round 2: 2 sc in each st. (8 sts)

Rounds 3 to 11: 1 sc in each st.

There is no need to stuff the snake.

Round 12: Press the opening with your fingers, aligning 4 sts side by side and sc both sides together by working 1 sc into each pair of sts.

Fasten off, leaving a long tail to sew to the crown.

Using **mint green** yarn, embroider eyes to the snake and fold the head forward. Secure it into position with a few stitches using your yarn needle.

STRAP 1 OF BELT

Row 1: Using **yellow** yarn, ch 9, 1 sc in the second ch from hook, 1 sc in each ch to end. (8 sts)

Fasten off, leaving a long tail to sew to the belt.

STRAP 2 OF BELT

Row 1: Using **yellow** yarn, ch 7, 1 sc in the second ch from hook, 1 sc in each ch to end. (6 sts)

Fasten off, leaving a long tail to sew to the belt.

ASSEMBLY

Sew the hair to the head *(see Techniques: Sewing the Hair)*.

Sew the snake to the crown, right in the middle of Cleopatra's forehead.

Sew the arms to the sides of the body *(see Techniques: Sewing the Arms)*.

Sew the straps to the belt, slightly towards the left.

Weave in all ends inside the doll.

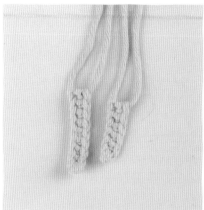

"I will not be triumphed over."

MATERIALS

2.5mm (C/2)
crochet hook

100% 8-ply cotton;
colours used: skin colour,
white, light blue, dark
blue, grey, dark grey,
brown, sage green, peach,
small amount of pink

Yarn needle

8mm (⅓in) safety eyes

Stitch marker

Fibrefill stuffing

FINISHED SIZE

20cm (7¾in) tall

EMMELINE PANKHURST

Why Emmeline? Because she dedicated her entire life to fighting for equality between men and women. And she knew that equality could start to be achieved if women were granted voting rights. She founded the Women's Social and Political Union (WSPU), whose members became known as suffragettes, and bravely led a series of rallies, demonstrations and even hunger strikes. Her bravery helped make other women aware of what was being denied them.

She soon she gathered hundreds of followers. When World War I broke out, Emmeline devoted her energies to supporting the war effort, encouraging women to take factory jobs so that men could fight on the front line. These contributions convinced the Government to grant voting rights to women over 30 in 1918. Later that year, another bill gave women the right to be elected to Parliament. Emmeline died on 14 June 1928; she did not live to see that shortly after her death women in the UK were granted full and equal voting rights with men, or that other countries followed suit.

LEG 1

Round 1: Using **skin** colour, 6 sc in a magic ring. (6 sts)

Round 2: 2 sc in each st. (12 sts)

Rounds 3 to 8: 1 sc in each st.

Round 9: Change to **white** for the underwear, 1 sc BLO in each st.

Fasten off. Set aside.

LEG 2

Work as for Leg 1, but do not fasten off yarn at the end. We will continue with the body.

BODY

Round 10: Still with leg 2 on your hook, ch 3 and join to leg 1 with a sc *(see Techniques: Joining Legs)*, place a stitch marker here for new beg of round, work 11 sc all along leg 1, 1 sc into each ch of 3-ch-loop, 12 sc all along leg 2 and 1 sc into other side of each ch of 3-ch-loop. (30 sts)

Round 11: *4 sc, 2 sc in the next st, rep from * to end. (36 sts)

Rounds 12 to 15: 1 sc in each st.

Round 16: Change to **skin** colour, 1 sc BLO in each st.

Stuff the legs firmly at this point.

Round 17: *4 sc, sc2tog, rep from * to end. (30 sts)

Round 18: Change to **light blue** yarn for the skirt, 1 sc in each st.

Round 19: Change to **dark grey** yarn for the belt, 1 sc BLO in each st.

Round 20: *3 sc, sc2tog, rep from * to end. (24 sts)

Round 21: Change to **white** yarn for the shirt, 1 sc BLO in each st.

Rounds 22 and 23: 1 sc in each st.

Round 24: *2 sc, sc2tog, rep from * to end. (18 sts)

Stuff the body firmly at this point.

Rounds 25 and 26: 1 sc in each st.

Round 27: *1 sc, sc2tog, rep from * to end. (12 sts)

Round 28: 1 sc BLO in each st.

Rounds 29 and 30: 1 sc in each st.

Round 31: Change to **skin** colour, 1 sc BLO in each st.

Do not fasten off yarn. We will continue with the head.

HEAD

Round 32: 2 sc in each st. (24 sts)

Round 33: *3 sc, 2 sc in the next st, rep from * to end. (30 sts)

Stuff the neck area firmly at this point.

Round 34: *4 sc, 2 sc in the next st, rep from * to end. (36 sts)

Round 35: *5 sc, 2 sc in the next st, rep from * to end. (42 sts)

Round 36: 1 sc in each st.

Round 37: 26 sc, 1 bobble st for the nose *(see Stitches: Bobble st)*, 1 sc in each st to end. Be sure to align the nose with the middle of the legs and adjust the positioning if necessary.

We will now start crocheting the collar of Emmeline's shirt, as it will be easier to do so without the finished head. Place a stitch marker in the loop on your hook to secure it and cut the yarn.

"We are here, not because we are law-breakers; we are here in our efforts to become law-makers..."

COLLAR

Turn the body upside down and join **white** yarn in one of the front loops of round 31, at the back of the neck.

Round 1: *1 sc, 2 sc in the next st, rep from * to end. (18 sts)

Round 2: *2 sc, 1 picot st *(see Stitches: Picot st)* on top of the previous st, rep from * to end. 1 slst in the first sc of the round to finish.

Fasten off and weave in ends.

We will now continue with the head. Rejoin the **skin** colour yarn to where you stopped working the head.

Rounds 38 to 46: 1 sc in each st.

Round 47: *5 sc, sc2tog, rep from * to end. (36 sts)

Start stuffing the head at this point.

Round 48: *4 sc, sc2tog, rep from * to end. (30 sts)

Place safety eyes one round above the nose, with 8 sts between them, embroider cheeks with **pink** yarn.

Round 49: *3 sc, sc2tog, rep from * to end. (24 sts)

Round 50: *2 sc, sc2tog, rep from * to end. (18 sts)

Stuff firmly.

Round 51: *1 sc, sc2tog, rep from * to end. (12 sts)

Round 52: (sc2tog) 6 times. (6 sts)

Fasten off and weave in ends.

SKIRT

Turn the body upside down and join **light blue** yarn in one of the front loops of round 19, at the back of the body.

Round 1: 1 sc FLO in each st of round 19. (30 sts)

Round 2: *4 sc, 2 sc in the next st, rep from * to end. (36 sts)

Round 3: 1 sc in each st.

Round 4: *5 sc, 2 sc in the next st, rep from * to end. (42 sts)

Rounds 5 to 7: 1 sc in each st.

Round 8: *6 sc, 2 sc in the next st, rep from * to end. (48 sts)

Rounds 9 to 14: 1 sc in each st.

Round 15: *7 sc, 2 sc in the next st, rep from * to end. (54 sts)

Rounds 16 and 17: 1 sc in each st.

Round 18: *8 sc, 2 sc in the next st, rep from * to end. (60 sts)

Round 19: *1 slst, 1 sc, (1 hdc, 1 dc, 1 hdc) all in the same st, 1 sc, 1 slst, rep from * to end. (84 sts)

Fasten off and weave in ends.

HAIR

Round 1: Using **brown** for the hair, 6 sc in a magic ring. (6 sts)

Round 2: 2 sc in each st. (12 sts)

Round 3: *1 sc, 2 sc in the next st, rep from * to end. (18 sts)

Round 4: *2 sc, 2 sc in the next st, rep from * to end. (24 sts)

Round 5: *3 sc, 2 sc in the next st, rep from * to end. (30 sts)

Round 6: *4 sc, 2 sc in the next st, rep from * to end. (36 sts)

Round 7: *5 sc, 2 sc in the next st, rep from * to end. (42 sts)

Round 8: *13 sc, 2 sc in the next st, rep from * to end. (45 sts)

Rounds 9 to 15: 1 sc in each st.

Round 16: *ch 9, 1 sc in the second ch from hook, 1 sc in each st along ch (8 sts), 1 sc, rep from * 24 times. Leave the rest of the stitches in the round unworked.

Fasten off, leaving a long tail to sew to the head.

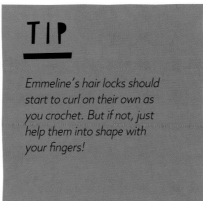

TIP

Emmeline's hair locks should start to curl on their own as you crochet. But if not, just help them into shape with your fingers!

ARMS (MAKE TWO)

Round 1: Using **skin** colour, ch 2, 4 sc in the second ch from hook. (4 sts)

Round 2: 2 sc in each st. (8 sts)

Rounds 3 to 5: 1 sc in each st.

Round 6: Change to **dark blue** yarn for the coat, 1 sc BLO in each st.

There is no need to stuff the arms.

Rounds 7 to 16: 1 sc in each st.

Round 17: Press the opening with your fingers, aligning 4 sts side by side and sc both sides together by working 1 sc into each pair of sts (see Techniques: Closing the Arms).

Fasten off, leaving a long tail to sew to the body.

COAT

The coat is actually a vest, but when you put it on your Emmeline, together with the arms, it will look like a coat. The vest is worked in rows. Use **dark blue**.

Row 1: Ch 21, 1 sc in the second ch from hook, 1 sc in each ch to end, ch 1, turn. (20 sts)

Row 2: 4 sc, *ch 6, skip the following 4 sts (to create armhole), 4 sc, rep from * once more, ch 1, turn.

Row 3: 4 sc, *6 sc in the 6-ch-loop, 4 sc, rep from * once more, ch 1, turn. (24 sts)

Rows 4 to 6: 1 sc in each st, ch 1, turn.

Row 7: 2 sc in the next st, 22 sc, 2 sc in the next st, ch 1, turn. (26 sts)

Row 8: 1 sc in each st, ch 1, turn.

Row 9: 2 sc in the next st, 24 sc, 2 sc in the next st, ch 1, turn. (28 sts)

Row 10: 1 sc in each st, ch 1, turn.

Row 11: 2 sc in the next st, 26 sc, 2 sc in the next st, ch 1, turn. (30 sts)

Rows 12 and 13: 1 sc in each st, ch 1, turn.

Row 14: 2 sc in the next st, 28 sc, 2 sc in the next st, ch 1, turn. (32 sts)

Rows 15 to 17: 1 sc in each st, ch 1, turn.

Row 18: 1 sc in each st, rotate the work 90 degrees clockwise and work 17 sc along the side of the vest, working in the spaces between rows. When you reach the top edge, crochet 20 slst in the remaining loops of the foundation chain. Then ch 1, rotate the piece 90 degrees clockwise again and work 18 sc along the other side of the vest, working in the spaces between rows. Work 1 slst in the first sc of row 18 to close (see Techniques: Edging of Flat pieces).

Fasten off and weave in ends.

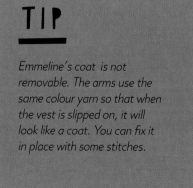

TIP

Emmeline's coat is not removable. The arms use the same colour yarn so that when the vest is slipped on, it will look like a coat. You can fix it in place with some stitches.

HAT

Round 1: Using **grey** for the hat, 6 sc in a magic ring. (6 sts)

Round 2: 2 sc in each st. (12 sts)

Round 3: 2 sc in each st. (24 sts)

Round 4: *3 sc, 2 sc in the next st, rep from * to end. (30 sts)

Round 5: *4 sc, 2 sc in the next st, rep from * to end. (36 sts)

Round 6: *5 sc, 2 sc in the next st, rep from * to end. (42 sts)

Round 7: *6 sc, 2 sc in the next st, rep from * to end. (48 sts)

Round 8: 1 sc BLO in each st.

Rounds 9 to 12: 1 sc in each st.

Round 13: Change to **dark grey**, 1 sc in each st.

Round 14: 1 sc in each st.

Fasten off and weave in ends.

RIM OF HAT

Turn the hat with the opening towards you and join **dark grey** yarn in one of the front loops of the last round of the hat.

Round 1: 1 sc FLO in each st of round 14 of the hat. (48 sts)

Round 2: 1 slst, 1 sc, 1 hdc, 8 dc, 1 hdc, 1 sc, 3 slst, 1 sc, 2 hdc, 3 dc, 2 hdc, 1 sc, 3 slst, 2 sc, 1 hdc, 12 dc, 1 hdc, 4 sc.

Fasten off and weave in ends.

FEATHERS (MAKE TWO)

Round 1: Using **sage green** yarn, ch 11, 1 sc in the second ch from hook, 1 slst, 2 sc, 3 hdc, 2 sc, 1 slst, 3 slst in the last st of the chain (this will allow you to turn and work on the other side of the chain), 1 slst, 2 sc, 3 hdc, 2 sc, 1 slst.

Close with a slst in the first stitch you've made. Fasten off, leaving a long tail to sew to the hat. Make another feather using **peach** yarn.

ASSEMBLY

Sew the hair to the head *(see Techniques: Sewing the Hair)*, with the short hair curls along Emmeline's forehead.

Sew the arms to the sides of the body *(see Techniques: Sewing the Arms)*, right below the collar of her shirt.

Slip the vest up her arms. It will look like a coat.

Sew the feathers to Emmeline's hat, in between the hat and the rim.

Place the hat on her head.

Weave in all ends inside the doll.

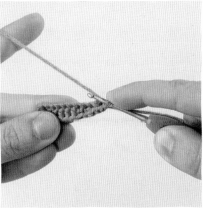

MATERIALS

FOR FLORENCE

2.5mm (C/2)
crochet hook

100% 8-ply cotton;
colours used: skin colour,
white, jeans blue, brown,
small amount of pink

Yarn needle

8mm (⅓in) safety eyes

Stitch marker

Fibrefill stuffing

FOR FLORENCE'S LAMP

2mm (B/1) crochet hook

100% 4-ply cotton;
colours used: yellow, black

FINISHED SIZE

FLORENCE

20cm (7¾in) tall

LAMP

3.5cm (1⅜in) tall

Please note that the lamp
is crocheted with a smaller
hook and thinner yarn.

FLORENCE NIGHTINGALE

Why Florence? Because to this day she remains the guiding light
of compassionate health care. Defying her parents' expectations,
she decided to pursue her true calling: a career in nursing. She took
jobs and volunteered in several hospitals, gaining experiences which
pushed her to seek improvements in hygiene conditions.

During the Crimean War, she organised a group of nurses to tend to
the sick and fallen soldiers, and she spent every waking minute caring
for her patients. At night she moved through the dark hallways
carrying a lamp, making sure the soldiers were safe and sound. This
is how she acquired her nickname: "The Lady of the Lamp".

Florence's work radically reduced the death count at that British
base hospital and, when she returned home, she was welcomed
as a hero. She founded the Nightingale Training School for Nurses
and published a book about her experiences in Crimea, using them
to advocate for the reform of the health-care system. Florence's
contributions during her long-serving life have shaped the way
hospitals work and are organised worldwide.

LEG 1

Round 1: Using **skin** colour, 6 sc in a magic ring. (6 sts)

Round 2: 2 sc in each st. (12 sts)

Rounds 3 to 8: 1 sc in each st.

Round 9: Change to **white** for the underwear, 1 sc BLO in each st.

Fasten off. Set aside.

LEG 2

Work as for Leg 1, but do not fasten off yarn at the end. We will continue with the body.

BODY

Round 10: Still with leg 2 on your hook, ch 3 and join to leg 1 with a sc *(see Techniques: Joining Legs)*, place a stitch marker here for new beg of round, work 11 sc all along leg 1, 1 sc into each ch of 3-ch-loop, 12 sc all along leg 2 and 1 sc into other side of each ch of 3-ch-loop. (30 sts)

Round 11: *4 sc, 2 sc in the next st, rep from * to end. (36 sts)

Rounds 12 to 16: 1 sc in each st.

Round 17: Change to **jeans blue** yarn for the skirt, *4 sc, sc2tog, rep from * to end. (30 sts)

Stuff the legs firmly at this point.

Round 18: Change to **white** yarn for the apron, 1 sc BLO in each st.

Round 19: 1 sc BLO in each st.

Round 20: 1 sc in each st.

Round 21: *3 sc, sc2tog, rep from * to end. (24 sts)

Rounds 22 and 23: 1 sc in each st.

Round 24: *2 sc, sc2tog, rep from * to end. (18 sts)

Stuff the body firmly at this point.

Round 25: Change to **jeans blue** yarn for the dress, 1 sc BLO in each st.

Round 26: 1 sc in each st.

Round 27: *1 sc, sc2tog, rep from * to end. (12 sts)

Round 28: 1 sc in each st.

Round 29: Change to **white** yarn for the collar, 1 sc in each st.

Round 30: Change to **skin** colour, 1 sc BLO in each st.

Round 31: 1 sc in each st.

Do not fasten off yarn. We will continue with the head.

HEAD

Round 32: 2 sc in each st. (24 sts)

Round 33: *3 sc, 2 sc in the next st, rep from * to end. (30 sts)

Stuff the neck area firmly at this point.

Round 34: *4 sc, 2 sc in the next st, rep from * to end. (36 sts)

Round 35: *5 sc, 2 sc in the next st, rep from * to end. (42 sts)

Round 36: 1 sc in each st.

Round 37: 26 sc, 1 bobble st for the nose *(see Stitches: Bobble st)*, 1 sc in each st to end. Be sure to align the nose with the middle of the legs and adjust the positioning if necessary.

We will now start crocheting the collar of Florence's dress, as it will be easier to do so without the finished head. Place a stitch marker in the loop on your hook to secure it and cut the yarn.

"The greatest heroes are those who do their duty in the daily grind of domestic affairs whilst the world whirls as a maddening dreidel.."

COLLAR

Turn the body upside down and join **white** yarn in one of the front loops of round 30, at the back of the neck.

Round 1: 1 sc FLO in each st. (12 sts)

Round 2: 4 sc, (1 hdc, 1 dc) in next st, (3 dc) in next st, 1 slst, (1 slst, ch 2, 2 dc in the base of the ch-2) in next st, (1 dc, 1 hdc) in next st, 3 sc.

Fasten off and weave in ends. We will now continue with the head. Rejoin the **skin** colour yarn to where you stopped working the head.

Rounds 38 to 46: 1 sc in each st.

Round 47: *5 sc, sc2tog, rep from * to end. (36 sts)

Start stuffing the head at this point.

Round 48: *4 sc, sc2tog, rep from * to end. (30 sts)

Place safety eyes one round above the nose, with 8 sts between them, embroider cheeks with **pink** yarn.

Round 49: *3 sc, sc2tog, rep from * to end. (24 sts)

Round 50: *2 sc, sc2tog, rep from * to end. (18 sts)

Stuff firmly.

Round 51: *1 sc, sc2tog, rep from * to end. (12 sts)

Round 52: (sc2tog) 6 times. (6 sts)

Fasten off and weave in ends.

SKIRT OF THE DRESS

Turn the body upside down and join **jeans blue** yarn in one of the front loops of round 18, at the back of the body.

Round 1: 1 sc FLO in each st of round 18. (30 sts)

Round 2: *4 sc, 2 sc in the next st, rep from * to end. (36 sts)

Round 3: 1 sc in each st.

Round 4: *5 sc, 2 sc in the next st, rep from * to end. (42 sts)

Rounds 5 to 7: 1 sc in each st.

Round 8: *6 sc, 2 sc in the next st, rep from * to end. (48 sts)

Rounds 9 to 12: 1 sc in each st.

Round 13: *7 sc, 2 sc in the next st, rep from * to end. (54 sts)

Rounds 14 to 17: 1 sc in each st.

Fasten off and weave in ends.

SKIRT OF THE APRON

Turn the body upside down and join **white** yarn in one of the front loops of round 19, at the back of the body.

Round 1: 1 sc FLO in each st of round 19. (30 sts)

Round 2: *4 sc, 2 sc in the next st, rep from * to end. (36 sts)

Round 3: 1 sc in each st.

Round 4: *5 sc, 2 sc in the next st, rep from * to end. (42 sts)

Rounds 5 to 7: 1 sc in each st.

Round 8: *6 sc, 2 sc in the next st, rep from * to end. (48 sts)

Rounds 9 and 10: 1 sc in each st.

Fasten off and weave in ends.

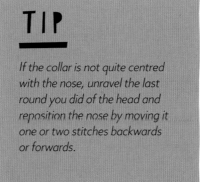

TIP

If the collar is not quite centred with the nose, unravel the last round you did of the head and reposition the nose by moving it one or two stitches backwards or forwards.

ARMS (MAKE TWO)

Round 1: Using **skin** colour, ch 2, 4 sc in the second ch from hook. (4 sts)

Round 2: 2 sc in each st. (8 sts)

Rounds 3 to 5: 1 sc in each st.

Round 6: Change to **jeans blue** yarn, 1 sc BLO in each st.

There is no need to stuff the arms.

Rounds 7 to 17: 1 sc in each st.

Round 18: Press the opening with your fingers, aligning 4 sts side by side and sc both sides together by working 1 sc into each pair of sts *(see Techniques: Closing the Arms)*.

Fasten off, leaving a long tail to sew to the body.

HAIR

Round 1: Using **brown** for the hair, 6 sc in a magic ring. (6 sts)

Round 2: 2 sc in each st. (12 sts)

Round 3: *1 sc, 2 sc in the next st, rep from * to end. (18 sts)

Round 4: *2 sc, 2 sc in the next st, rep from * to end. (24 sts)

Round 5: *3 sc, 2 sc in the next st, rep from * to end. (30 sts)

Round 6: *4 sc, 2 sc in the next st, rep from * to end. (36 sts)

Round 7: *5 sc, 2 sc in the next st, rep from * to end. (42 sts)

Round 8: *13 sc, 2 sc in the next st, rep from * to end. (45 sts)

Rounds 9 to 15: 1 sc in each st.

Round 16: 1 slst, 1 sc, 1 hdc, 12 dc, 1 hdc, 1 sc, 1 slst, 1 sc, 1 hdc, 12 dc, 1 hdc, 1 sc, 1 slst, *ch 11, 1 sc in the second ch from hook, 1 sc in each st along ch, 1 slst, rep from * to last st. (10 short hair curls)

Fasten off, leaving a long tail to sew to the head.

NURSE CAP

Round 1: Using **white** for the cap, 6 sc in a magic ring. (6 sts)

Round 2: 2 sc in each st. (12 sts)

Round 3: *1 sc, 2 sc in the next st, rep from * to end. (18 sts)

Round 4: *2 sc, 2 sc in the next st, rep from * to end. (24 sts)

Round 5: *3 sc, 2 sc in the next st, rep from * to end. (30 sts)

Round 6: *4 sc, 2 sc in the next st, rep from * to end. (36 sts)

Round 7: *5 sc, 2 sc in the next st, rep from * to end. (42 sts)

Round 8: *6 sc, 2 sc in the next st, rep from * to end. (48 sts)

Round 9: *7 sc, 2 sc in the next st, rep from * to end. (54 sts)

Round 10: *8 sc, 2 sc in the next st, rep from * to end. (60 sts)

Rounds 11 to 13: 1 sc in each st.

Round 14: *8 sc, sc2tog, rep from * to end. (54 sts)

Round 15: *7 sc, sc2tog, rep from * to end. (48 sts)

Round 16: 1 sc BLO in each st.

Round 17: 1 sc in each st.

Round 18: *2 sc, 1 picot st *(see Stitches: Picot st)* on top of the previous st, rep from * to end. 1 slst in the first sc of the round to finish.

Fasten off and weave in ends.

ASSEMBLY

Sew the hair to the head (see Techniques: Sewing the Hair).

Sew the arms to the sides of the body (see Techniques: Sewing the Arms).

Place the nurse cap on Florence's head.

Weave in all ends inside the doll.

NIGHT LAMP

IMPORTANT! This lamp is crocheted using the smaller hook of 2mm (US B/1) and the 4-ply yarn.

GLASS

Round 1: Using **yellow**, 6 sc in a magic ring. (6 sts)

Round 2: 2 sc in each st. (12 sts)

Round 3: *1 sc, 2 sc in the next st, rep from * to end. (18 sts)

Round 4: 1 sc BLO in each st.

Rounds 5 to 12: 1 sc in each st.

Round 13: 1 sc BLO in each st.

Round 14: *1 sc, sc2tog, rep from * to end. (12 sts)

Round 15: (sc2tog) 6 times. (6 sts)

Fasten off and weave in ends.

BLACK LID/BASE (MAKE TWO)

Round 1: Using **black**, 6 sc in a magic ring. (6 sts)

Round 2: 2 sc in each st. (12 sts)

Round 3: *1 sc, 2 sc in the next st, rep from * to end. (18 sts)

Round 4: *2 sc, 2 sc in the next st, rep from * to end. (24 sts)

Round 5: 1 sc BLO in each st.

Round 6: 1 sc in each st.

Fasten off, leaving a long tail for sewing.

HANDLE

Using black yarn and leaving a long tail at the beginning, ch 12. Fasten off leaving a long tail for sewing.

ASSEMBLY

Sew the lid and the base to the top and bottom of the glass. And before cutting the remaining yarn tails, embroider some lines across the glass.

Using a yarn needle, sew the handle to the top of the lid of the lamp.

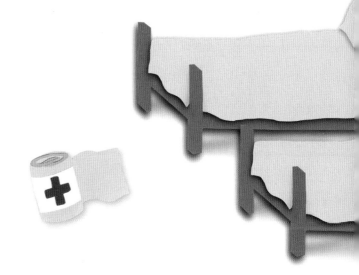

MATERIALS

2.5mm (C/2)
crochet hook

100% 8-ply cotton;
colours used: skin colour,
white, light blue, light
grey, light yellow, brown,
small amount of pink

Yarn needle

8mm (⅓in) safety eyes

Stitch marker

Fibrefill stuffing

FINISHED SIZE

20cm (7¾in) tall

GRETA THUNBERG

Why Greta? Because she is an ordinary teenage girl who did the extraordinary: she simply chose to care, leaving her childhood behind in order to raise awareness of climate change. Thanks to her Fridays For Future strikes, the world began to listen. Within a year her tireless campaigning against environmental depredation had gone global. Sometimes all it takes is just one person - that person was Greta. She defied world leaders, went viral on social media and sparked an international youth movement seeking immediate answers. Joined by millions of other boys and girls, and backing up her arguments with scientific evidence, she has given a voice to an entire generation.

LEG 1

Round 1: Using **light blue** yarn for the jeans, 6 sc in a magic ring. (6 sts)

Round 2: 2 sc in each st. (12 sts)

Rounds 3 to 9: 1 sc in each st

Fasten off. Set aside.

LEG 2

Work as for Leg 1, but do not fasten off yarn at the end. We will continue with the body.

BODY

Round 10: Still with leg 2 on your hook, ch 3 and join to leg 1 with a sc *(see Techniques: Joining Legs)*, place a stitch marker here for new beg of round, work 11 sc all along leg 1, 1 sc into each ch of 3 ch loop, 12 sc all along leg 2 and 1 sc into other side of each ch of 3-ch-loop. (30 sts)

Round 11: *4 sc, 2 sc in the next st, rep from * to end. (36 sts)

Rounds 12 to 16: 1 sc in each st.

Round 17: *4 sc, sc2tog, rep from * to end. (30 sts)

Round 18: Change to **skin** colour, 1 sc BLO in each st.

Stuff the legs firmly at this point.

Rounds 19 and 20: 1 sc in each st.

Round 21: *3 sc, sc2tog, rep from * to end. (24 sts)

Rounds 22 and 23: 1 sc in each st.

Round 24: *2 sc, sc2tog, rep from * to end. (18 sts)

Stuff the body firmly at this point.

Rounds 25 and 26: 1 sc in each st.

Round 27: *1 sc, sc2tog, rep from * to end. (12 sts)

Round 28: Change to **white** yarn for the t-shirt, 1 sc in each st.

Round 29: Change to **light grey** yarn for the collar of the t-shirt, 1 sc BLO in each st.

Round 30: 1 sc in each st.

Round 31: Change to **skin** colour, 1 sc BLO in each st.

Do not fasten off yarn. We will continue with the head.

HEAD

Round 32: 2 sc in each st. (24 sts)

Round 33: *3 sc, 2 sc in the next st, rep from * to end. (30 sts)

Stuff the neck area firmly at this point.

Round 34: *4 sc, 2 sc in the next st, rep from * to end. (36 sts)

Round 35: *5 sc, 2 sc in the next st, rep from * to end. (42 sts)

Round 36: 1 sc in each st.

Round 37: 26 sc, 1 bobble st for the nose *(see Stitches: Bobble st)*, 1 sc in each st to end. Be sure to align the nose with the middle of the legs and adjust the positioning if necessary.

We will now start crocheting Greta's t-shirt, as it will be easier to do so without the finished head. Place a stitch marker in the loop on your hook to secure it and cut the yarn.

T-SHIRT

Turn the body upside down and join **white** yarn in one of the front loops of round 29, at the back of the neck.

Round 1: 1 sc FLO in each st of round 29. (12 sts)

Round 2: *1 sc, 2 sc in the next st, rep from * to end. (18 sts)

Round 3: 1 sc in each st.

Round 4: *2 sc, 2 sc in the next st, rep from * to end. (24 sts)

Rounds 5 to 7: 1 sc in each st.

Round 8: *3 sc, 2 sc in the next st, rep from * to end. (30 sts)

Rounds 9 and 10: 1 sc in each st.

Round 11: *4 sc, 2 sc in the next st, rep from * to end. (36 sts)

Rounds 12 to 14: 1 sc in each st.

Round 15: *8 sc, 2 sc in the next st, rep from * to end. (40 sts)

Rounds 16 and 17: 1 sc in each st.

Fasten off and weave in ends.

We will now continue with the head. Rejoin the **skin** colour yarn to where you stopped working the head.

Rounds 38 to 46: 1 sc in each st.

Round 47: *5 sc, sc2tog, rep from * to end. (36 sts)

Start stuffing the head at this point.

Round 48: *4 sc, sc2tog, rep from * to end. (30 sts)

Place safety eyes one round above the nose, with 8 sts between them, embroider cheeks with **pink** yarn.

Round 49: *3 sc, sc2tog, rep from * to end. (24 sts)

Round 50: *2 sc, sc2tog, rep from * to end. (18 sts)

Stuff firmly.

Round 51: *1 sc, sc2tog, rep from * to end. (12 sts)

Round 52: (sc2tog) 6 times. (6 sts)

Fasten off and weave in ends.

HAIR

Round 1: Using **brown** for the hair, 6 sc in a magic ring. (6 sts)

Round 2: 2 sc in each st. (12 sts)

Round 3: *1 sc, 2 sc in the next st, rep from * to end. (18 sts)

Round 4: *2 sc, 2 sc in the next st, rep from * to end. (24 sts)

Round 5: *3 sc, 2 sc in the next st, rep from * to end. (30 sts)

Round 6: *4 sc, 2 sc in the next st, rep from * to end. (36 sts)

Round 7: *5 sc, 2 sc in the next st, rep from * to end. (42 sts)

Round 8: *13 sc, 2 sc in the next st, rep from * to end. (45 sts)

Rounds 9 to 15: 1 sc in each st.

Round 16: 1 slst, 1 sc, 1 hdc, 10 dc, 1 hdc, 1 sc, 1 slst, 1 sc, 1 hdc, 10 dc, 1 hdc, 1 sc, 1 slst, leave the rest of the stitches unworked

Fasten off, leaving a long tail to sew to the head. Sew the hair piece to Greta's head now. When reaching the forehead, make a few stitches to simulate some loose hairs.

BRAID

Cut **9 strands** of 28cm (11in) each using your **brown** yarn. Choose three stitches right in the centre of the back of Greta's head, on the edge of the hair piece. With your yarn needle, pass three strands through each stitch, folding them in halves. Take the strands and braid them. Tie them with a bit of the **light blue** yarn used for her jeans. Trim the ends to make the braid tidier.

ARMS (MAKE TWO)

Round 1: Using **skin** colour, ch 2, 4 sc in the second ch from hook. (4 sts)

Round 2: 2 sc in each st. (8 sts)

Rounds 3 to 5: 1 sc in each st.

Round 6: Change to **light yellow** yarn for the hoodie, 1 sc BLO in each st.

There is no need to stuff the arms.

Rounds 7 to 17: 1 sc in each st.

Round 18: Press the opening with your fingers, aligning 4 sts side by side and sc both sides together by working 1 sc into each pair of sts *(see Techniques: Closing the Arms)*.

Fasten off, leaving a long tail to sew to the body.

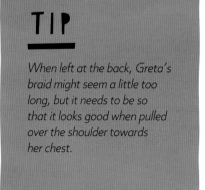

TIP

When left at the back, Greta's braid might seem a little too long, but it needs to be so that it looks good when pulled over the shoulder towards her chest.

GRETA'S HOODIE

The hoodie is actually a vest, but when you put it on your Greta, together with the arms, it will look like a hoodie. The vest is worked in rows. Use **light yellow**.

Row 1: Ch 21, 1 sc in the second ch from hook, 1 sc in each ch to end, ch 1, turn. (20 sc)

Row 2: 4 sc, *ch 6, skip the following 4 sts (to create armhole), 4 sc, rep from * once more, ch 1, turn.

Row 3: 4 sc, *6 sc in the 6-ch-loop, 4 sc, rep from * once more, ch 1, turn. (24 sts)

Rows 4 to 14: 1 sc in each st, ch 1, turn.

Row 15: 1 sc in each st, ch 1, rotate the work 90 degrees clockwise and work 15 sc along the side of the vest, working in the spaces between rows. When you reach the top edge, crochet 20 slst in the remaining loops of the foundation chain. Then ch 1, rotate the piece 90 degrees clockwise again and work 15 sc along the other side of the vest, working in the spaces between rows *(see Techniques: Edging of Flat Pieces)*.

Fasten off and weave in ends.

HOOD OF THE HOODIE

Join **light yellow** yarn, with a slip knot, in the upper right corner of the vest piece.

The hood is also crocheted in rows.

Row 1: 1 sc in each st of the upper edge of the vest, ch 1, turn. (20 sts)

Row 2: *1 sc, 2 sc in the next st, rep from * to end, ch 1, turn. (30 sts)

Row 3: *2 sc, 2 sc in the next st, rep from * to end, ch 1, turn. (40 sts)

Rows 4 to 19: 1 sc in each st, ch 1, turn.

Careful! The hood changes a bit here. Now we are going to create a little slant.

Row 20: 1 sc in the next 20 sts, ch 1, turn. Leave the rest of the stitches of the row unworked.

Row 21: sc2tog, 18 sc, ch 1, turn.

Row 22: 17 sc, sc2tog, ch 1, turn.

Row 23: sc2tog, 16 sc, ch 1, turn.

Row 24: 15 sc, sc2tog, ch 1, turn.

Row 25: sc2tog, 14 sc, ch 1, turn.

Fasten off and weave in ends.

We now need to mirror what we have done on the other side of the hood. Insert the **light yellow** yarn, with a slip knot, in the other corner. We will continue working in rows.

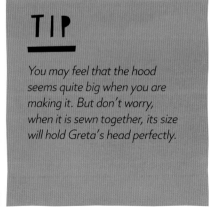

TIP

You may feel that the hood seems quite big when you are making it. But don't worry, when it is sewn together, its size will hold Greta's head perfectly.

Row 1: 1 sc in the following 20 sts, ch 1, turn.

Row 2: sc2tog, 18 sc, ch 1, turn.

Row 3: 17 sc, sc2tog, ch 1, turn.

Row 4: sc2tog, 16 sc, ch 1, turn.

Row 5: 15 sc, sc2tog, ch 1, turn.

Row 6: sc2tog, 14 sc, ch 1, turn.

Fasten off, leaving a long tail to close the hood.

Fold the two sides together, so that the seams line up. Thread the remaining yarn tail with your yarn needle and sew together both sides, to close the hood.

Once the top of the hood is closed, insert the **light yellow** yarn with a slip stitch right where the vest and the hood meet and work a series of sc along the opening of the hood, working in between the rows, for a tidier finish.

ASSEMBLY

Sew the arms to the sides of the body *(see Techniques: Sewing the Arms)*.

Pull on the **light yellow** vest with the hood through the arms. Together with the arms, it will look like a hoodie. You can fix it in place with a few stitches.

Make sure to bring the braid to the front, towards Greta's chest, as she wears it.

Weave in all ends inside the doll.

"I have learned you are never too small to make a difference."

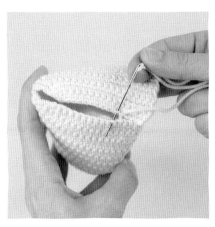  

MATERIALS

2.5mm (C/2)
crochet hook

100% 8-ply cotton;
colours used: skin colour,
white, baby blue, dark
grey, brown, beige,
small amount of pink

Yarn needle

8mm (⅓in) safety eyes

Stitch marker

Fibrefill stuffing

FINISHED SIZE

20cm (7¾in) tall

JANE AUSTEN

Why Jane? Because she is one of the most beloved writers around the world and her novels have become literary classics, still attracting new fans and inspiring many TV and cinema adaptations. She was witty and creative, smart and curious, and had a sharp eye for detail - perfectly describing the society of her time. During her life all her novels were published anonymously. It was after she died that she received the acclaim she so richly deserved. And today, 200 years after her death, the love stories she imagined, with such passion and social insight, are still very much up to date.

LEG 1

Round 1: Using **skin** colour, 6 sc in a magic ring. (6 sts)

Round 2: 2 sc in each st. (12 sts)

Rounds 3 to 8: 1 sc in each st.

Round 9: Change to **white** for the underwear, 1 sc BLO in each st.

Fasten off. Set aside.

LEG 2

Work as for Leg 1, but do not fasten off yarn at the end. We will continue with the body.

BODY

Round 10: Still with leg 2 on your hook, ch 3 and join to leg 1 with a sc (see Techniques: Joining Legs), place a stitch marker here for new beg of round, work 11 sc all along leg 1, 1 sc into each ch of 3-ch-loop, 12 sc all along leg 2 and 1 sc into other side of each ch of 3-ch-loop. (30 sts)

Round 11: *4 sc, 2 sc in the next st, rep from * to end. (36 sts)

Rounds 12 to 15: 1 sc in each st.

Round 16: Change to **skin** colour, 1 sc BLO in each st.

Stuff the legs firmly at this point.

Round 17: 1 sc in each st.

Round 18: *4 sc, sc2tog, rep from * to end. (30 sts)

Round 19: Change to **baby blue** yarn for the dress, 1 sc in each st.

Round 20: Change to **dark grey** yarn for the belt, 1 sc BLO in each st.

Round 21: *3 sc, sc2tog, rep from * to end. (24 sts)

Round 22: Change back to **baby blue** yarn for the dress, 1 sc BLO in each st.

Round 23: 1 sc in each st.

Round 24: *2 sc, sc2tog, rep from * to end. (18 sts)

Stuff the body firmly at this point.

Rounds 25: 1 sc in each st.

Round 26: Change to **skin** colour, 1 sc BLO in each st.

Round 27: *1 sc, sc2tog, rep from * to end. (12 sts)

Rounds 28 to 31: 1 sc in each st.

Do not fasten off yarn. We will continue with the head.

HEAD

Round 32: 2 sc in each st. (24 sts)

Round 33: *3 sc, 2 sc in the next st, rep from * to end. (30 sts)

Stuff the neck area firmly at this point.

Round 34: *4 sc, 2 sc in the next st, rep from * to end. (36 sts)

Round 35: *5 sc, 2 sc in the next st, rep from * to end. (42 sts)

Round 36: 1 sc in each st.

Round 37: 20 sc, 1 bobble st for the nose (see Stitches: Bobble st), 1 sc in each st to end. Be sure to align the nose with the middle of the legs and adjust the positioning if necessary.

Rounds 38 to 46: 1 sc in each st.

Round 47: *5 sc, sc2tog, rep from * to end. (36 sts)

Start stuffing the head at this point.

Round 48: *4 sc, sc2tog, rep from * to end. (30 sts)

Place safety eyes one round above the nose, with 8 sts between them, embroider cheeks with **pink** yarn.

Round 49: *3 sc, sc2tog, rep from * to end. (24 sts)

Round 50: *2 sc, sc2tog, rep from * to end. (18 sts)

Stuff firmly.

Round 51: *1 sc, sc2tog, rep from * to end. (12 sts)

Round 52: (sc2tog) 6 times. (6 sts)

Fasten off and weave in ends.

"I wish, as well as everybody else, to be perfectly happy; but, like everybody else, it must be in my own way."
From "Sense and Sensibility", spoken by Elinor Dashwood.

SKIRT OF JANE'S REGENCY DRESS

Turn the body upside down and join **baby blue** yarn in one of the front loops of round 20, at the back of the body.

Round 1: 1 sc in each front loops of round 20. (30 sts)

Round 2: 1 sc in each st.

Round 3: *4 sc, 2 sc in the next st, rep from * to end. (36 sts)

Rounds 4 to 7: 1 sc in each st.

Round 8: *5 sc, 2 sc in the next st, rep from * to end. (42 sts)

Rounds 9 to 13: 1 sc in each st.

Round 14: *6 sc, 2 sc in the next st, rep from * to end. (48 sts)

Rounds 15 to 21: 1 sc in each st.

Fasten off and weave in ends.

ARMS (MAKE TWO)

Round 1: Using **skin** colour, ch 2, 4 sc in the second ch from hook. (4 sts)

Round 2: 2 sc in each st. (8 sts)

Rounds 3 to 12: 1 sc in each st.

Round 13: Change to **baby blue** yarn, 2 sc BLO in each st. (16 sts)

There is no need to stuff the arms.

Rounds 14 to 16: 1 sc in each st.

Round 17: (sc2tog) 8 times. (8 sts)

Round 18: Press the opening with your fingers, aligning 4 sts side by side and sc both sides together by working 1 sc into each pair of sts *(see Techniques: Closing the Arms)*.

Fasten off, leaving a long tail to sew to the body.

HAIR

Round 1: Using **brown** for the hair, 6 sc in a magic ring. (6 sts)

Round 2: 2 sc in each st. (12 sts)

Round 3: *1 sc, 2 sc in the next st, rep from * to end. (18 sts)

Round 4: *2 sc, 2 sc in the next st, rep from * to end. (24 sts)

Round 5: *3 sc, 2 sc in the next st, rep from * to end. (30 sts)

Round 6: *4 sc, 2 sc in the next st, rep from * to end. (36 sts)

Round 7: *5 sc, 2 sc in the next st, rep from * to end. (42 sts)

Round 8: *13 sc, 2 sc in the next st, rep from * to end. (45 sts)

Rounds 9 to 15: 1 sc in each st.

Round 16: *1 slst, ch 11, 1 sc in the second ch from hook, 1 sc in each st along ch (10 sts), rep from * 3 times, 1 slst, 1 sc, 1 hdc, 1 dc, 1 hdc, 1 sc, 1 slst, 1 sc, 1 hdc, 1 dc, 1 hdc, 1 sc, 1 slst, *ch 11, 1 sc in the second ch from hook, 1 sc in each st along ch (10 sts), 1 slst, rep from * 3 times. Leave the rest of the stitches in the round unworked.

Fasten off, leaving a long tail to sew to the head.

TIP

Jane's hair locks should curl naturally as you crochet, but if they don't, help them into shape with your fingers.

HAIRBUN

Round 1: Using **brown**, 6 sc in a magic ring. (5 sts)

Round 2: 2 sc in each st. (10 sts)

Round 3: *1 sc, 2 sc in the next st, rep from * to end. (15 sts)

Round 4: *2 sc, 2 sc in the next st, rep from * to end. (20 sts)

Rounds 5 to 7: 1 sc in each st.

Round 8: Change to **baby blue** yarn, 1 sc in each st.

Fasten off, leaving a long tail to sew to the head.

BONNET

Round 1: Using **baby blue** yarn for the bonnet, 6 sc in a magic ring. (6 sts)

Round 2: 2 sc in each st. (12 sts)

Round 3: *1 sc, 2 sc in the next st, rep from * to end. (18 sts)

Round 4: *2 sc, 2 sc in the next st, rep from * to end. (24 sts)

Round 5: *3 sc, 2 sc in the next st, rep from * to end. (30 sts)

Round 6: 1 sc BLO in each st.

Rounds 7 and 8: 1 sc in each st.

Round 9: *4 sc, 2 sc in the next st, rep from * to end. (36 sts)

Rounds 10 and 11: 1 sc in each st.

Round 12: *5 sc, 2 sc in the next st, rep from * to end. (42 sts)

Round 13: 1 sc in each st.

Round 14: *6 sc, 2 sc in the next st, rep from * to end. (48 sts)

Rounds 15 and 16: 1 sc in each st.

Round 17: Change to **dark grey** yarn for the ribbon, 1 sc BLO in each st.

Round 18: 1 sc in each st.

Round 19: Change back to **baby blue** yarn and work in BLO: 15 sc, *2 sc in the next st, 1 sc, rep from * 9 times, 15 sc. (57 sts)

Round 20: 15 sc, 1 hdc, *4 dc, 2 dc in the next st, rep from * 5 times, 1 hdc, 15 sc. (62 sts)

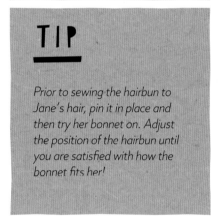

TIP

Prior to sewing the hairbun to Jane's hair, pin it in place and then try her bonnet on. Adjust the position of the hairbun until you are satisfied with how the bonnet fits her!

SHAWL

The shawl is crocheted in rows.

Row 1: Using **beige** yarn, ch 51, 1 sc in the second ch from hook, 1 sc in each ch to end. (50 sts)

Rows 2 to 5: Ch 1, turn, 1 sc BLO in each st.

Fasten off and weave in ends.

ASSEMBLY

Sew the hair to the head *(see Techniques: Sewing the Hair)*, with the curls in line with Jane's eyes.

Stuff and sew the hairbun to her hair, right in the middle.

Sew the arms to the sides of the body *(see Techniques: Sewing the Arms)*.

Cover Jane's arms with the shawl. Fix it in place with a nice pin or a few stitches.

Weave in all ends inside the doll.

TIP

You can add a fringe to each end of Jane's shawl. Or you can replace it all together with a nice piece of fabric, even dare to embroider it with some flowers.

MATERIALS

2.5mm (C/2)
crochet hook

100% 8-ply cotton;
colours used: skin colour,
blue, light grey, black,
small amount of pink

Yarn needle

8mm (⅓in) safety eyes

Stitch marker

Fibrefill stuffing

A piece of fabric 43cm
(17in) by 15cm (5¾in)
to cover Malala's head

FINISHED SIZE

20cm (7¾in) tall

MALALA YOUSAFZAI

Why Malala? Because when she was denied the right to study by
the Taliban in Pakistan, she was not afraid to defy them and fight
for her rights and those of other girls. They responded with a death
threat and Malala was subsequently shot in the head by a Taliban
gunman in 2012. She survived after many struggles but was not
able to return to her dear home country. Nonetheless she went on
advocating for free, safe and quality education for girls, placing the
spotlight on the many abuses suffered under terrorist regimes. In
2014 Malala became the youngest person to receive the Nobel
Peace Prize at the tender age of 17.

LEG 1

Round 1: Using **blue** yarn for the pants, 6 sc in a magic ring. (6 sts)

Round 2: 2 sc in each st. (12 sts)

Rounds 3 to 9: 1 sc in each st.

Fasten off. Set aside.

LEG 2

Work as for Leg 1, but do not fasten off yarn at the end. We will continue with the body.

BODY

Round 10: Still with leg 2 on your hook, ch 3 and join to leg 1 with a sc *(see Techniques: Joining Legs)*, place a stitch marker here for new beg of round, work 11 sc all along leg 1, 1 sc into each ch of 3-ch-loop, 12 sc all along leg 2 and 1 sc into other side of each ch of 3-ch-loop. (30 sts)

Round 11: *4 sc, 2 sc in the next st, rep from * to end. (36 sts)

Rounds 12 to 16: 1 sc in each st.

Round 17: *4 sc, sc2tog, rep from * to end. (30 sts)

Round 18: Change to **skin** colour, 1 sc BLO in each st.

Stuff the legs firmly at this point.

Rounds 19 and 20: 1 sc in each st.

Round 21: *3 sc, sc2tog, rep from * to end. (24sts)

Rounds 22 and 23: 1 sc in each st.

Round 24: *2 sc, sc2tog, rep from * to end. (18 sts)

Stuff the body firmly at this point.

Rounds 25 and 26: 1 sc in each st.

Round 27: *1 sc, sc2tog, rep from * to end. (12 sts)

Round 28: Change to **light grey** yarn for the tunic-shirt, 1 sc in each st.

Round 29: Change to **blue** yarn for the collar of the tunic-shirt, 1 sc BLO in each st.

Round 30: 1 sc in each st.

Round 31: Change to **skin** colour, 1 sc BLO in each st.

Do not fasten off yarn. We will continue with the head.

HEAD

Round 32: 2 sc in each st. (24 sts)

Round 33: *3 sc, 2 sc in the next st, rep from * to end. (30 sts)

Stuff the neck area firmly at this point.

Round 34: *4 sc, 2 sc in the next st, rep from * to end. (36 sts)

Round 35: *5 sc, 2 sc in the next st, rep from * to end. (42 sts)

Round 36: 1 sc in each st.

Round 37: 26 sc, 1 bobble st for the nose *(see Stitches: Bobble st)*, 1 sc in each st to end. Be sure to align the nose with the middle of the legs and adjust the positioning if necessary.

We will now start crocheting Malala's tunic-shirt, as it will be easier to do so without the finished head. Place a stitch marker in the loop on your hook to secure it and cut the yarn.

"I have the right of education. I have the right to play. I have the right to sing. I have the right to talk. I have the right to go to market. I have the right to speak up."

TUNIC-SHIRT

Turn the body upside down and join **light grey** yarn in one of the front loops of round 29, at the back of the neck.

Round 1: 1 sc FLO in each st of round 29. (12 sts)

Round 2: *1 sc, 2 sc in the next st, rep from * to end. (18 sts)

Round 3: 1 sc in each st.

Round 4: *2 sc, 2 sc in the next st, rep from * to end. (24 sts)

Rounds 5 to 7: 1 sc in each st.

Round 8: *3 sc, 2 sc in the next st, rep from * to end. (30 sts)

Rounds 9 and 10: 1 sc in each st.

Round 11: *4 sc, 2 sc in the next st, rep from * to end. (36 sts)

Rounds 12 to 14: 1 sc in each st.

Round 15: *5 sc, 2 sc in the next st, rep from * to end. (42 sts)

Rounds 16 to 19: 1 sc in each st.

Round 20: Change to **blue** yarn, 1 sc in each st.

Round 21: Change back to **light grey**, 1 sc in each st.

Fasten off and weave in ends.

We will now continue with the head. Rejoin the **skin** colour yarn to where you stopped working the head.

Rounds 38 to 46: 1 sc in each st.

Round 47: *5 sc, sc2tog, rep from * to end. (36 sts)

Start stuffing the head at this point.

Round 48: *4 sc, sc2tog, rep from * to end. (30 sts)

Place safety eyes one round above the nose, with 8 sts between them, embroider cheeks with **pink** yarn.

Round 49: *3 sc, sc2tog, rep from * to end. (24 sts)

Round 50: *2 sc, sc2tog, rep from * to end. (18 sts)

Stuff firmly.

Round 51: *1 sc, sc2tog, rep from * to end. (12 sts)

Round 52: (sc2tog) 6 times. (6 sts)

Fasten off and weave in ends.

TIP

Malala likes colourful clothes, so if you choose a colour-block headscarf, you could also add some embroidery or coloured beads to her short tunic!

ARMS (MAKE TWO)

Round 1: Using **skin** colour, ch 2, 4 sc in the second ch from hook. (4 sts)

Round 2: 2 sc in each st. (8 sts)

Rounds 3 to 5: 1 sc in each st.

Round 6: Change to **blue** yarn, 1 sc BLO in each st.

There is no need to stuff the arms.

Round 7: 1 sc in each st.

Round 8: Change to **light gray** yarn, 1 sc in each st.

Rounds 9 to 17: 1 sc in each st.

Round 18: Press the opening with your fingers, aligning 4 sts side by side and sc both sides together by working 1 sc into each pair of sts *(see Techniques: Closing the Arms)*.

Fasten off, leaving a long tail to sew to the body.

HAIR

Round 1: Using **black** for the hair, 6 sc in a magic ring. (6 sts)

Round 2: 2 sc in each st. (12 sts)

Round 3: *1 sc, 2 sc in the next st, rep from * to end. (18 sts)

Round 4: *2 sc, 2 sc in the next st, rep from * to end. (24 sts)

Round 5: *3 sc, 2 sc in the next st, rep from * to end. (30 sts)

Round 6: *4 sc, 2 sc in the next st, rep from * to end. (36 sts)

Round 7: *5 sc, 2 sc in the next st, rep from * to end. (42 sts)

Round 8: *13 sc, 2 sc in the next st, rep from * to end. (45 sts)

Rounds 9 to 15: 1 sc in each st.

Round 16: 1 slst, 1 sc, 1 hdc, 12 dc, 1 hdc, 1 sc, 1 slst, 1 sc, 1 hdc, 8 dc, 1 hdc, 1 sc, 1 slst, *1 slst in next st, ch 21, 1 sc in the second ch from hook, 1 sc in each st along ch (20 sts), rep from * to last st, 1 slst. (14 hair curls)

Fasten off, leaving a long tail to sew to the head.

TIP

Malala's hair locks should curl naturally. But if they don't, you can help them into a shape with your fingers, like a corkscrew.

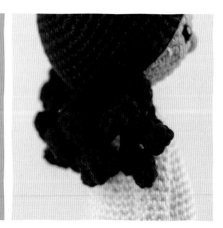

ASSEMBLY

Sew the hair to the head *(see Techniques: Sewing the Hair)*. Malala's hair is parted slightly to the right.

Sew the arms to the sides of the body *(see Techniques: Sewing the Arms)*.

Cover Malala's head with the scarf, following the instructions below. You can secure it in place with a few stitches.

Weave in all ends inside the doll.

HOW TO COVER MALALA'S HEAD

Take the piece of fabric and place it over Malala's head, covering her hair.

Then wrap the end on the left over the shoulder on the right and pin it or stitch it to Malala's back.

The end on the right should stay on her chest.

"Let us pick up our books and our pens, they are the most powerful weapons."

MATERIALS

FOR MARIE

2.5mm (C/2)
crochet hook

100% 8-ply cotton;
colours used: skin colour,
white, dark grey, brown,
small amount of pink

Yarn needle

8mm (⅓in) safety eyes

Stitch marker

Fibrefill stuffing

FOR MARIE'S FLASK

2mm (B/1) crochet hook

100% 4-ply cotton;
colours used:
green, light blue

Fibrefill stuffing

FINISHED SIZE

MARIE

20cm (7¾in) tall

FLASK

3cm (1¼in) tall

Please note that the flask
is crocheted with a smaller
hook and thinner yarn.

MARIE CURIE

Why Marie? Because she still is a role model for all scientists. She was smart and talented and made many efforts to be able to study science when only men could do so. And she excelled. When she discovered radioactivity, her husband Pierre, also a scientist, left his investigations to help Marie with her research. Together they discovered polonium and radium. Marie was the first woman to receive a Nobel Prize (Physics). In fact, she won two (also Chemistry), being the first person to ever achieve this. After Pierre's death, she helped to develop the use of X-rays in medicine. She was an advocate for using knowledge for good and her example opened the door to many other women willing to pursue a career in science.

LEG 1

Round 1: Using **skin** colour, 6 sc in a magic ring. (6 sts)

Round 2: 2 sc in each st. (12 sts)

Rounds 3 to 8: 1 sc in each st.

Round 9: Change to **white** for the underwear, 1 sc BLO in each st.

Fasten off. Set aside.

LEG 2

Work as for Leg 1, but do not fasten off yarn at the end. We will continue with the body.

BODY

Round 10: Still with leg 2 on your hook, ch 3 and join to leg 1 with a sc *(see Techniques: Joining Legs)*, place a stitch marker here for new beg of round, work 11 sc all along leg 1, 1 sc into each ch of 3-ch-loop, 12 sc all along leg 2 and 1 sc into other side of each ch of 3-ch-loop. (30 sts)

Round 11: *4 sc, 2 sc in the next st, rep from * to end. (36 sts)

Rounds 12 to 15: 1 sc in each st.

Round 16: Change to **skin** colour, 1 sc BLO in each st.

Stuff the legs firmly at this point.

Round 17: *4 sc, sc2tog, rep from * to end. (30 sts)

Round 18: Change to **dark grey** yarn for the skirt, 1 sc in each st.

Round 19: 1 sc BLO in each st.

Round 20: *3 sc, sc2tog, rep from * to end. (24 sts)

Rounds 21 to 23: 1 sc in each st.

Round 24: *2 sc, sc2tog, rep from * to end. (18 sts)

Stuff the body firmly at this point.

Rounds 25 and 26: 1 sc in each st.

Round 27: *1 sc, sc2tog, rep from * to end. (12 sts)

Round 28: 1 sc in each st.

Round 29: 1 sc BLO in each st.

Rounds 30 and 31: 1 sc in each st.

Do not fasten off yarn. We will continue with the head.

HEAD

Round 32: Change to **skin** colour, 2 sc in each st. (24 sts)

Round 33: *3 sc, 2 sc in the next st, rep from * to end. (30 sts)

Stuff the neck area firmly at this point.

Round 34: *4 sc, 2 sc in the next st, rep from * to end. (36 sts)

Round 35: *5 sc, 2 sc in the next st, rep from * to end. (42 sts)

Round 36: 1 sc in each st.

Round 37: 26 sc, 1 bobble st for the nose *(see Stitches: Bobble st)*, 1 sc in each st to end. Be sure to align the nose with the middle of the legs and adjust the positioning if necessary.

We will now start crocheting the collar of Marie's dress, as it will be easier to do so without the finished head. Place a stitch marker in the loop on your hook to secure it and cut the yarn.

"I am one of those who think, like Nobel, that humanity will draw more good than evil from new discoveries."

COLLAR

Turn the body upside down and join **dark grey** yarn in one of the front loops of round 29, at the back of the neck.

Round 1: *1 sc, 2 sc in the next st, rep from * to end. (18 sts)

Round 2: *2 sc, 2 sc in the next st, rep from * to end. (24 sts)

Round 3: 1 sc in each st.

Round 4: *2 sc, 1 picot st (see Stitches: Picot st) on top of the previous st rep from * 12 times. 1 slst in the first sc of the round to finish.

Fasten off and weave in ends.

We will now continue with the head. Rejoin the **skin** colour yarn to where you stopped working the head.

Rounds 38 to 46: 1 sc in each st.

Round 47: *5 sc, sc2tog, rep from * to end. (36 sts)

Start stuffing the head at this point.

Round 48: *4 sc, sc2tog, rep from * to end. (30 sts)

Place safety eyes one round above the nose, with 8 sts between them, embroider cheeks with **pink** yarn.

Round 49: *3 sc, sc2tog, rep from * to end. (24 sts)

Round 50: *2 sc, sc2tog, rep from * to end. (18 sts)

Stuff firmly.

Round 51: *1 sc, sc2tog, rep from * to end. (12 sts)

Round 52: (sc2tog) 6 times. (6 sts)

Fasten off and weave in ends.

SKIRT

Turn the body upside down and join **dark grey** yarn in one of the front loops of round 19, at the back of the body.

Round 1: 1 sc FLO in each st of round 19. (30 sts)

Round 2: *4 sc, 2 sc in the next st, rep from * to end. (36 sts)

Round 3: 1 sc in each st.

Round 4: *5 sc, 2 sc in the next st, rep from * to end. (42 sts)

Rounds 5 to 7: 1 sc in each st.

Round 8: *6 sc, 2 sc in the next st, rep from * to end. (48 sts)

Rounds 9 to 14: 1 sc in each st.

Round 15: *7 sc, 2 sc in the next st, rep from * to end. (54 sts)

Rounds 16 to 18: 1 sc in each st.

Fasten off and weave in ends.

ARMS (MAKE TWO)

Round 1: Using **skin** colour, ch 2, 4 sc in the second ch from hook. (4 sts)

Round 2: 2 sc in each st. (8 sts)

Rounds 3 to 5: 1 sc in each st.

Round 6: Change to **dark grey**, 1 sc BLO in each st.

There is no need to stuff the arms.

Rounds 7 to 16: 1 sc in each st.

Round 17: Press the opening with your fingers, aligning 4 sts side by side and sc both sides together by working 1 sc into each pair of sts (see Techniques: Closing the Arms).

Fasten off, leaving a long tail to sew to the body.

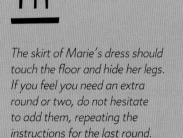

TIP

The skirt of Marie's dress should touch the floor and hide her legs. If you feel you need an extra round or two, do not hesitate to add them, repeating the instructions for the last round.

TIP

The hair curls on Marie's forehead need to be parted, six to one side and six to the other. Position them with your fingers and they should remain in place.

HAIR

Round 1: Using **brown** for the hair, 6 sc in a magic ring. (6 sts)

Round 2: 2 sc in each st. (12 sts)

Round 3: *1 sc, 2 sc in the next st, rep from * to end. (18 sts)

Round 4: *2 sc, 2 sc in the next st, rep from * to end. (24 sts)

Round 5: *3 sc, 2 sc in the next st, rep from * to end. (30 sts)

Round 6: *4 sc, 2 sc in the next st, rep from * to end. (36 sts)

Round 7: *5 sc, 2 sc in the next st, rep from * to end. (42 sts)

Round 8: *13 sc, 2 sc in the next st, rep from * to end. (45 sts)

Rounds 9 to 15: 1 sc in each st.

Round 16: *ch 9, 1 sc in the second ch from hook, 1 sc in each st along ch (8 sts), 2 sc, rep from * 12 times. Leave the rest of the stitches in the round unworked.

Fasten off, leaving a long tail to sew to the head.

HAIRBUN

Round 1: Using **brown**, 6 sc in a magic ring. (6 sts)

Round 2: 2 sc in each st. (12 sts)

Round 3: *1 sc, 2 sc in the next st, rep from * to end. (18 sts)

Round 4: *2 sc, 2 sc in the next st, rep from * to end. (24 sts)

Rounds 5 to 8: 1 sc in each st.

Round 9: *2 sc, sc2tog, rep from * to end. (18 sts)

Fasten off, leaving a long tail to sew to the head.

MARIE'S ERLENMEYER FLASK

IMPORTANT! This laboratory flask is crocheted using the smaller hook of 2mm (US B/1) and the 4-ply yarn.

Round 1: Using **green**, 6 sc in a magic ring. (6 sts)

Round 2: 2 sc in each st. (12 sts)

Round 3: *1 sc, 2 sc in the next st, rep from * to end. (18 sts)

Round 4: *2 sc, 2 sc in the next st, rep from * to end. (24 sts)

Round 5: 1 sc BLO in each st.

Round 6: *2 sc, sc2tog, rep from * to end. (18 sts)

Round 7: 1 sc in each st.

Start stuffing at this point, but only the lower half of the flask.

Round 8: *1 sc, sc2tog, rep from * to end. (12 sts)

Round 9: Change to **light blue**, 1 sc in each st.

Round 10: 1 sc in each st.

Round 11: *1 sc, sc2tog, rep from * to end. (8 sts)

Rounds 12 and 13: 1 sc in each st.

Round 14: 2 sc in each st. (16 sts)

Close with slst in next st, fasten off and weave in ends.

ASSEMBLY

Sew the hair to the head *(see Techniques: Sewing the Hair)*, parting 6 hair curls to one side and 6 to the other.

Stuff and sew the hairbun to Marie's hair.

Sew the arms to the sides of the body *(see Techniques: Sewing the Arms)*, right below the collar of her dress (you will have to lift it to do so).

Sew the Erlenmeyer flask to Marie's hands.

Weave in all ends inside your doll.

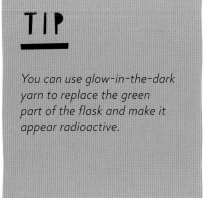

TIP

You can use glow-in-the-dark yarn to replace the green part of the flask and make it appear radioactive.

"Life is not easy for any of us. But what of that? We must have perseverance and above all confidence in ourselves. We must believe that we are gifted for something and that this thing must be attained."

MATERIALS

2.5mm (C/2)
crochet hook

100% 8-ply cotton;
colours used: skin
colour, white, sage
green, steel blue, light
blue, black, brown,
small amount of pink

Yarn needle

8mm (⅓in) safety eyes

Stitch marker

Fibrefill stuffing

20cm (7¾in) of black
coated wire for Rosa's
glasses and pliers

Craft glue or black
sewing thread

FINISHED SIZE

20cm (7¾in) tall

ROSA PARKS

Why Rosa? Because she was a fighter for human equality. And in a time of segregation, she was not afraid to stand up for her rights. After she was taken to jail for denying her seat on the bus to a white person in Montgomery, Alabama, she led a year-long boycott of buses, which was the dawning of a nationwide movement to end segregation in public facilities in the United States. Her efforts and suffering transformed her into one of the leaders of the civil rights movement, a "job" she kept her entire life, inspiring others with her dignity and bravery. She was awarded the Martin Luther King Jr. Award, the Presidential Medal of Freedom and the Congressional Gold Medal.

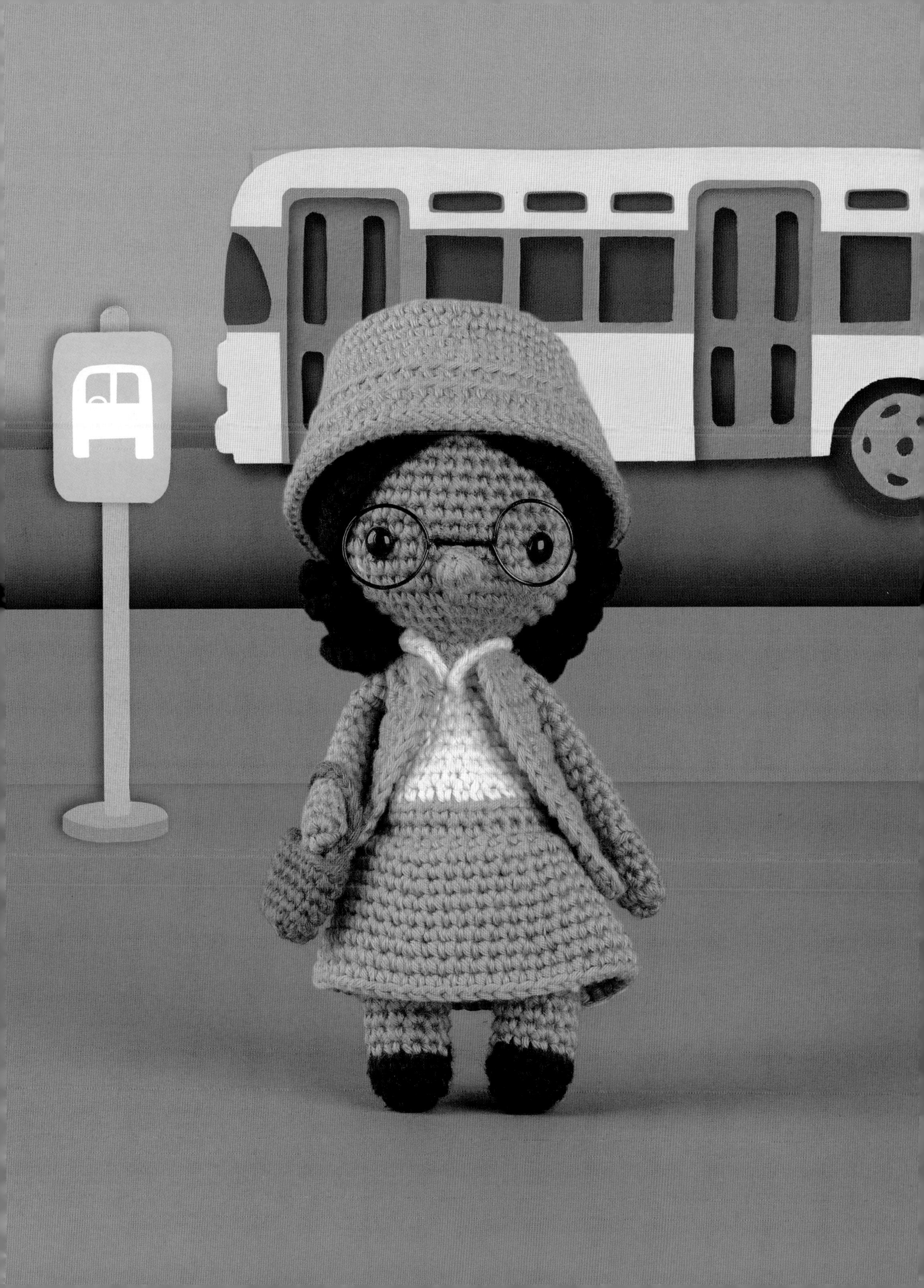

LEG 1

Round 1: Using **black** yarn for the shoes, 6 sc in a magic ring. (6 sts)

Round 2: 2 sc in each st. (12 sts)

Rounds 3 and 4: 1 sc in each st.

Round 5: Change to **skin** colour, 1 sc BLO in each st.

Rounds 6 to 8: 1 sc in each st.

Round 9: Change to **white** for the underwear, 1 sc BLO in each st.

Fasten off. Set aside.

LEG 2

Work as for Leg 1, but do not fasten off yarn at the end. We will continue with the body.

BODY

Round 10: Still with leg 2 on your hook, ch 3 and join to leg 1 with a sc *(see Techniques: Joining Legs)*, place a stitch marker here for new beg of round, work 11 sc all along leg 1, 1 sc into each ch of 3-ch-loop, 12 sc all along leg 2 and 1 sc into other side of each ch of 3-ch-loop. (30 sts)

Round 11: *4 sc, 2 sc in the next st, rep from * to end. (36 sts)

Rounds 12 to 15: 1 sc in each st.

Round 16: Change to **skin** colour, 1 sc BLO in each st.

Stuff the legs firmly at this point.

Round 17: Change to **sage green** yarn for the skirt, *4 sc, sc2tog, rep from * to end. (30 sts)

Round 18: 1 sc BLO in each st.

Round 19: 1 sc in each st.

Round 20: Change to **light blue** yarn for the shirt, 1 sc BLO in each st.

Round 21: *3 sc, sc2tog, rep from * to end. (24 sts)

Rounds 22 and 23: 1 sc in each st.

Round 24: *2 sc, sc2tog, rep from * to end. (18 sts)

Stuff the body firmly at this point.

Rounds 25 and 26: 1 sc in each st.

Round 27: *1 sc, sc2tog, rep from * to end. (12 sts)

Round 28: 1 sc in each st.

Round 29: 7 sc, change to **skin** colour, 1 sc, change back to **light blue**, 4 sc.

Round 30: 6 sc, change to **skin** colour, 3 sc, change back to **light blue**, 3 sc.

Round 31: 5 sc, change to **skin** colour, 5 sc, change back to **light blue**, 2 sc.

You should have a **skin** colour triangle at the front centre of the doll. Do not fasten off yarn.

We will continue with the head.

"You must never be fearful about what you are doing when it is right."

HEAD

Round 32: Change to **skin** colour, 2 sc BLO in each of the first 5 sts (those in **light blue**), 2 sc through both loops in each of the following 5 sts (those in **skin** colour), 2 sc BLO in each of last 2 sts (those in **light blue**). (24 sts)

Round 33: *3 sc, 2 sc in the next st, rep from * to end. (30 sts)

Stuff the neck area firmly at this point.

Round 34: *4 sc, 2 sc in the next st, rep from * to end. (36 sts)

Round 35: *5 sc, 2 sc in the next st, rep from * to end. (42 sts)

Round 36: 1 sc in each st.

Round 37: 26 sc, 1 bobble st for the nose (see Stitches: Bobble st), 1 sc in each st to end. Be sure to align the nose with the middle of the legs and adjust the positioning if necessary.

We will take a break here from the head to work the collar of Rosa's shirt. Place a stitch marker in the loop on your hook to secure.

For detailed photographs of how to work a collar see Techniques: Creating the V Collar.

Join the **light blue** yarn 2 rounds below the tip of the **skin** triangle. Work in the spaces between sts and crochet 2 surface sc up until you reach the bottom tip of the triangle.

Now follow the diagonal of the triangle, working the right side first. Crochet 1 surface sc in between each round, inserting the hook in the spaces between rounds, until you reach the round where the **light blue** front loops are showing.

Now crochet 2 sc in each front loop of the shirt bordering Rosa's neck, until you reach the edge of the triangle on the other side (14 sc). Work 5 surface sc in between rounds following the diagonal of the triangle to the starting stitch, work 1 slst in the starting stitch.

Fasten off and weave in ends.

We will now continue with the head. Rejoin the **skin** colour yarn to where you stopped working the head.

Rounds 38 to 46: 1 sc in each st.

Round 47: *5 sc, sc2tog, rep from * to end. (36 sts)

Start stuffing the head at this point.

Round 48: *4 sc, sc2tog, rep from * to end. (30 sts)

Place safety eyes one round above the nose, with 8 sts between them, embroider cheeks with **pink** yarn.

Round 49: *3 sc, sc2tog, rep from * to end. (24 sts)

Round 50: *2 sc, sc2tog, rep from * to end. (18 sts)

Stuff firmly.

Round 51: *1 sc, sc2tog, rep from * to end. (12 sts)

Round 52: (sc2tog) 6 times. (6 sts)

Fasten off and weave in ends.

SKIRT

Turn the body upside down and join **sage green** yarn in one of the front loops of round 18, at the back of the body.

Round 1: 1 sc FLO in each st of round 18. (30 sts)

Round 2: *4 sc, 2 sc in the next st, rep from * to end. (36 sts)

Round 3: 1 sc in each st.

Round 4: *5 sc, 2 sc in the next st, rep from * to end. (42 sts)

Rounds 5 to 7: 1 sc in each st.

Round 8: *6 sc, 2 sc in the next st, rep from * to end. (48 sts)

Rounds 9 and 10: 1 sc in each st.

Fasten off and weave in ends.

TIP

If you don't want to do Rosa's collar with surface single crochet, just embroider two diagonal lines using the colour of her shirt, to mark the edges of the skin triangle showing on her neck.

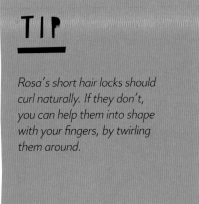

TIP

Rosa's short hair locks should curl naturally. If they don't, you can help them into shape with your fingers, by twirling them around.

HAIR

Round 1: Using **black** for the hair, 6 sc in a magic ring. (6 sts)

Round 2: 2 sc in each st. (12 sts)

Round 3: *1 sc, 2 sc in the next st, rep from * to end. (18 sts)

Round 4: *2 sc, 2 sc in the next st, rep from * to end. (24 sts)

Round 5: *3 sc, 2 sc in the next st, rep from * to end. (30 sts)

Round 6: *4 sc, 2 sc in the next st, rep from * to end. (36 sts)

Round 7: *5 sc, 2 sc in the next st, rep from * to end. (42 sts)

Round 8: *13 sc, 2 sc in the next st, rep from * to end. (45 sts)

Rounds 9 to 15: 1 sc in each st.

Round 16: 1 slst, 1 sc, 1 hdc, 10 dc, 1 hdc, 1 sc, 1 slst, 1 sc, 1 hdc, 10 dc, 1 hdc, 1 sc, 1 slst, *ch 11, 1 sc in the second ch from hook, 1 sc in each st along ch, 1 slst, rep from * to last st. (14 short hair curls)

Fasten off, leaving a long tail to sew to the head.

ARMS (MAKE TWO)

Round 1: Using **skin** colour, ch 2, 4 sc in the second ch from hook. (4 sts)

Round 2: 2 sc in each st. (8 sts)

Rounds 3 to 5: 1 sc in each st.

Round 6: Change to **steel blue** yarn for the coat, 1 sc BLO in each st.

There is no need to stuff the arms.

Rounds 7 to 16: 1 sc in each st.

Round 17: Press the opening with your fingers, aligning 4 sts side by side and sc both sides together by working 1 sc into each pair of sts *(see Techniques: Closing the Arms).*

Fasten off, leaving a long tail to sew to the body.

JACKET

The jacket is actually a vest, but when you put it on your Rosa, together with the arms, it will look like a jacket. The vest is worked in rows. Use **steel blue**.

Row 1: Ch 21, 1 sc in the second ch from hook, 1 sc in each ch to end, ch 1, turn. (20 sc)

Row 2: 4 sc, *ch 6, skip the following 4 sts (to create armhole), 4 sc, rep from * once more, ch 1, turn.

Row 3: 4 sc, *6 sc in the 6-ch-loop, 4 sc, rep from * once more, ch 1, turn. (24 sts)

Rows 4 to 14: 1 sc in each st, ch 1, turn.

Row 15: 1 sc in each st, ch 1, rotate the work 90 degrees clockwise and work 14 sc along the side of the vest, working in the spaces between rows. When you reach the top edge, crochet 20 slst in the remaining loops of the foundation chain. Then ch 1, rotate the piece 90 degrees clockwise again and work 15 sc along the other side of the vest, working in the spaces between rows *(see Techniques: Edging of Flat Pieces).*

Fasten off and weave in ends.

HAT

Round 1: Using **sage green** for the hat, 6 sc in a magic ring. (6 sts)

Round 2: 2 sc in each st. (12 sts)

Round 3: 2 sc in each st. (24 sts)

Round 4: *3 sc, 2 sc in the next st, rep from * to end. (30 sts)

Round 5: *4 sc, 2 sc in the next st, rep from * to end. (36 sts)

Round 6: *5 sc, 2 sc in the next st, rep from * to end. (42 sts)

Round 7: 1 sc in each st

Round 8: 1 sc BLO in each st

Round 9: 1 sc in each st

Round 10: *6 sc, 2 sc in the next st, rep from * to end. (48 sts)

Round 11: 1 sc in each st.

Round 12: *23 sc, 2 sc in the next st, rep from * twice. (50 sts)

Round 13: 1 sc in each st.

Round 14: 1 sc BLO in each st.

Round 15: 1 sc in each st.

Round 16: In BLO work: *1 sc, 2 sc in the next st, rep from * to end. (75 sts)

Round 17: 1 sc in each st.

Round 18: 1 slst in each st.

Fasten off and weave in ends.

ASSEMBLY

Sew the hair to the head *(see Techniques: Sewing the Hair)*.

Sew the arms to the sides of the body *(see Techniques: Sewing the Arms)*.

Slip the vest up Rosa's arms. It will look like a jacket.

Place the hat on her head.

Make Rosa's glasses *(see Techniques: Making Glasses)* and use craft glue to stick glasses over the nose. You can also sew them using a bit of **black** thread.

Weave in all ends inside the doll.

PURSE

Round 1: Using **brown** yarn, ch 7, 2 sc in the second ch from hook, 1 sc in each of next 4 ch, 4 sc in last ch, turn and work on the other side of the foundation chain, 1 sc in each of next 4 ch, 2 sc in last ch. (16 sts)

Rounds 2 to 6: 1 sc in each st.

Fasten off and weave in ends.

PURSE STRAP

Using **brown** yarn and leaving a long tail at the beginning, ch 15.

Fasten off leaving a long tail.

Using a yarn needle, sew the strap to the purse using both tails.

TIP

Using brown yarn, crochet a purse for your Rosa. Slide it over one hand and secure in place with a few stitches if desired.

MATERIALS

2.5mm (C/2)
crochet hook

100% 8-ply cotton;
colours used: skin colour,
dark grey, light grey,
black, brown, white,
small amount of pink

Yarn needle

8mm (⅓in) safety eyes

Stitch marker

Fibrefill stuffing

20cm (7¾in) of black
coated wire for Ruth's
glasses and pliers

Craft glue or black
sewing thread

2 green glass or plastic
beads for Ruth's earrings

FINISHED SIZE

20cm (7¾in) tall

RUTH BADER GINSBURG

Why Ruth? Ruth Bader Ginsburg was the first to question the legislation discriminating on the basis of sex, after constantly suffering unfair treatment for being a woman. At Harvard University, she was one of eight women studying law in a class of more than 500. She later transferred to Columbia University and graduated first in her class but, despite her outstanding academic record, no one would give her a job as a lawyer. This was the spark that ignited her passion to fight for gender-blind laws granting equal rights to everyone. She argued six landmark cases on gender equality before the US Supreme Court, winning five.

Ruth was a trailblazer who fought for gender equality, civil rights and the fair treatment of women and men.

LEG 1

Round 1: Using **dark grey** yarn for the pants, 6 sc in a magic ring. (6 sts)

Round 2: 2 sc in each st. (12 sts)

Rounds 3 to 9: 1 sc in each st.

Fasten off. Set aside.

LEG 2

Work as for Leg 1, but do not fasten off yarn at the end. We will continue with the body.

BODY

Round 10: Still with leg 2 on your hook, ch 3 and join to leg 1 with a sc *(see Techniques: Joining Legs)*, place a stitch marker here for new beg of round, work 11 sc all along leg 1, 1 sc into each ch of 3-ch-loop, 12 sc all along leg 2 and 1 sc into other side of each ch of 3-ch-loop. (30 sts)

Round 11: *4 sc, 2 sc in the next st, rep from * to end. (36 sts)

Rounds 12 to 16: 1 sc in each st.

Round 17: *4 sc, sc2tog, rep from * to end. (30 sts)

Round 18: Change to **light grey** yarn for the shirt, 1 sc BLO in each st.

Stuff the legs firmly at this point.

Rounds 19 and 20: 1 sc in each st.

Round 21: *3 sc, sc2tog, rep from * to end. (24sts)

Rounds 22 and 23: 1 sc in each st.

Round 24: *2 sc, sc2tog, rep from * to end. (18 sts)

Stuff the body firmly at this point.

Rounds 25 and 26: 1 sc in each st.

Round 27: *1 sc, sc2tog, rep from * to end. (12 sts)

Round 28: Change to **black** yarn for the robe, 1 sc in each st.

Round 29: 1 sc BLO in each st.

Round 30: 1 sc in each st.

Round 31: Change to **skin** colour, 1 sc BLO in each st.

Do not fasten off yarn. We will continue with the head.

HEAD

Round 32: 2 sc in each st. (24 sts)

Round 33: *3 sc, 2 sc in the next st, rep from * to end. (30 sts)

Stuff the neck area firmly at this point.

Round 34: *4 sc, 2 sc in the next st, rep from * to end. (36 sts)

Round 35: *5 sc, 2 sc in the next st, rep from * to end. (42 sts)

Round 36: 1 sc in each st.

Round 37: 26 sc, 1 bobble st for the nose *(see Stitches: Bobble st)*, 1 sc in each st to end. Be sure to align the nose with the middle of the legs and adjust the positioning if necessary.

We will now start crocheting Ruth's Supreme Court robe, as it will be easier to do so without the finished head. Place a stitch marker in the loop on your hook to secure it and cut the yarn.

TIP

The skirt of Ruth's dress should touch the floor and hide her legs. If you feel you need an extra round or two, do not hesitate to add them, repeating the instructions for the last round.

ROBE

Turn the body upside down and join **black** yarn in one of the front loops of round 29, at the back of the neck.

Round 1: 1 sc FLO in each st of round 29. (12 sts)

Round 2: *1 sc, 2 sc in the next st, rep from * to end. (18 sts)

Round 3: 1 sc in each st.

Round 4: *2 sc, 2 sc in the next st, rep from * to end. (24 sts)

Rounds 5 to 7: 1 sc in each st.

Round 8: *3 sc, 2 sc in the next st, rep from * to end. (30 sts)

Rounds 9 and 10: 1 sc in each st.

Round 11: *4 sc, 2 sc in the next st, rep from * to end. (36 sts)

Rounds 12 to 14: 1 sc in each st.

Round 15: *5 sc, 2 sc in the next st, rep from * to end. (42 sts)

Rounds 16 to 18: 1 sc in each st.

Round 19: *6 sc, 2 sc in the next st, rep from * to end. (48 sts)

Rounds 20 to 31: 1 sc in each st.

Fasten off and weave in ends.

We will now continue with the head. Rejoin the **skin** colour yarn to where you stopped working the head.

Rounds 38 to 46: 1 sc in each st.

Round 47: *5 sc, sc2tog, rep from * to end. (36 sts)

Start stuffing the head at this point.

Round 48: *4 sc, sc2tog, rep from * to end. (30 sts)

Place safety eyes one round above the nose, with 8 sts between them, embroider cheeks with **pink** yarn.

Round 49: *3 sc, sc2tog, rep from * to end. (24 sts)

Round 50: *2 sc, sc2tog, rep from * to end. (18 sts)

Stuff firmly.

Round 51: *1 sc, sc2tog, rep from * to end. (12 sts)

Round 52: (sc2tog) 6 times. (6 sts)

Fasten off and weave in ends.

EARS (MAKE TWO)

Round 1: Using **skin** colour, 6 sc in a magic ring. (6 sts)

Close the ring with a slst into the first sc and fasten off, leaving a long tail to sew to the head.

"I try to teach through my opinions, through my speeches, how wrong it is to judge people on the basis of what they look like, colour of their skin, whether they're men or women."

ARMS (MAKE TWO)

Round 1: Using **skin** colour, ch 2, 4 sc in the second ch from hook.

Round 2: 2 sc in each st. (8 sts)

Rounds 3 to 10: 1 sc in each st.

Round 11: Change to **black** yarn, 1 sc in each st.

There is no need to stuff the arms.

Round 12: 1 sc BLO in each st

Rounds 13 to 17: 1 sc in each st.

Round 18: Press the opening with your fingers, aligning 4 sts side by side and sc both sides together by working 1 sc into each pair of sts *(see Techniques: Closing the Arms).*

Fasten off, leaving a long tail to sew to the body.

SLEEVES

Join the **black** yarn in one of the remaining **front loops** of round 12 of one of the arms.

Round 1: 1 sc FLO in each st of round 12. (8 sts)

Round 2: *1 sc, 2 sc in the next st, rep from * to end. (12 sts)

Round 3: 1 sc in each st.

Round 4: *3 sc, 2 sc in the next st, rep from * to end. (15 sts)

Rounds 5 to 8: 1 sc in each st.

Fasten off and weave in ends. Repeat the sleeve with the other arm.

HAIR

Round 1: Using **brown** for the hair, 6 sc in a magic ring. (6 sts)

Round 2: 2 sc in each st. (12 sts)

Round 3: *1 sc, 2 sc in the next st, rep from * to end. (18 sts)

Round 4: *2 sc, 2 sc in the next st, rep from * to end. (24 sts)

Round 5: *3 sc, 2 sc in the next st, rep from * to end. (30 sts)

Round 6: *4 sc, 2 sc in the next st, rep from * to end. (36 sts)

Round 7: *5 sc, 2 sc in the next st, rep from * to end. (42 sts)

Round 8: *13 sc, 2 sc in the next st, rep from * to end. (45 sts)

Rounds 9 to 15: 1 sc in each st.

Round 16: 1 slst, 1 sc, 1 hdc, 14 dc, 1 hdc, 1 sc, 1 slst, 1 sc, 1 hdc, 6 dc, 1 hdc, 1 sc, 1 slst. Leave the rest of the stitches unworked.

Fasten off, leaving a long tail to sew to the head.

PONYTAIL LOCKS (MAKE THREE)

Row 1: Using **brown** yarn, ch 11, 1 sc in the second ch from hook, 1 sc in each ch to end. (10 sts)

Fasten off, leaving a long tail to sew to the head.

WHITE COLLAR

Row 1: Using **white** yarn and leaving a long tail at the beginning, ch 22, 1 sc in the second ch from hook, 1 sc in each ch to end, ch1, turn. (21 sts)

Row 2: Ch 5, skip the following 2 sts, 1 slst in the third stitch, *ch 6, skip the following 2 sts, 1 slst in the third stitch, rep from * 6 times.

Fasten off, leaving a long tail to knot around the neck. With your yarn needle, thread one of the ends and do some stitches to slim the edges.

ASSEMBLY

Sew the hair to the head *(see Techniques: Sewing the Hair)*. Ruth's hair is parted slightly to the right.

Sew the locks of hair to the back of the hair, to simulate her short ponytail. Tie them together with a bit of **black** yarn.

Sew the ears to the sides of the head. Sew one **green** bead to each ear as earrings.

Sew the arms to the sides of the robe *(see Techniques: Sewing the Arms)*.

Tie the collar around Ruth's neck.

Make Ruth's glasses *(see Techniques: Making Glasses)* and use craft glue to stick glasses over the nose. You can also sew them using a bit of **black** thread.

Weave in all ends inside the doll.

TIP

Ruth loved her necklaces, jabots and collars to be big, bold and attention grabbing. So be creative and don't be afraid to try beads or coloured yarns.

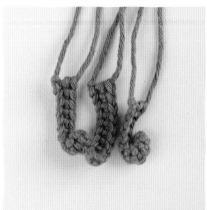

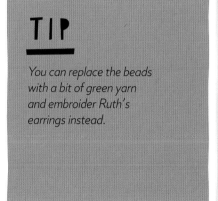

TIP

You can replace the beads with a bit of green yarn and embroider Ruth's earrings instead.

MATERIALS

2.5mm (C/2)
crochet hook

100% 8-ply cotton;
colours used: skin colour,
white, light purple, black,
small amount of pink

Yarn needle

8mm (⅓in) safety eyes

Stitch marker

Fibrefill stuffing

FINISHED SIZE

20cm (7¾in) tall

SERENA WILLIAMS

Why Serena? Because she is a stellar tennis player, has won 23
Grand Slam singles titles and multiple Olympic gold medals, and
holds several world records. She is a hard-working, hard-training
athlete who, together with her sister Venus, developed a signature
style of powerful playing that overwhelmed their opponents. But
above all, she has an immense capacity for overcoming obstacles
and setbacks; whether they be hard tournaments or physical
injuries, she is able to adjust her mindset and start over, with
amazing comebacks.

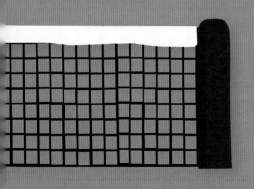

LEG 1

Round 1: Using **black** yarn for the tennis shoes, 6 sc in a magic ring. (6 sts)

Round 2: 2 sc in each st. (12 sts)

Round 3: 1 sc in each st.

Round 4: Change to **white** for the socks, 1 sc BLO in each st.

Round 5: Change to **skin** colour, 1 sc BLO in each st.

Rounds 6 to 8: 1 sc in each st.

Round 9: Change to **light purple** for the underwear, 1 sc BLO in each st.

Fasten off. Set aside.

LEG 2

Work as for Leg 1, but do not fasten off yarn at the end. We will continue with the body.

BODY

Round 10: Still with leg 2 on your hook, ch 3 and join to leg 1 with a sc *(see Techniques: Joining Legs)*, place a stitch marker here for new beg of round, work 11 sc all along leg 1, 1 sc into each ch of 3-ch-loop, 12 sc all along leg 2 and 1 sc into other side of each ch of 3-ch-loop. (30 sts)

Round 11: *4 sc, 2 sc in the next st, rep from * to end. (36 sts)

Rounds 12 to 16: 1 sc in each st.

Stuff the legs firmly at this point.

Round 17: *4 sc, sc2tog, rep from * to end. (30 sts)

Round 18: Change to **black** yarn for the belt, 1 sc BLO in each st.

Round 19: 1 sc in each st.

Round 20: Change to **light purple** yarn for the tennis suit, 1 sc BLO in each st.

Round 21: *3 sc, sc2tog, rep from * to end. (24 sts)

Rounds 22 and 23: 1 sc in each st.

Round 24: *2 sc, sc2tog, rep from * to end. (18 sts)

Stuff the body firmly at this point.

Rounds 25 to 27: 1 sc in each st.

Round 28: *1 sc, sc2tog, rep from * to end. (12 sts)

Rounds 29 to 31: 1 sc in each st.

Do not fasten off yarn. We will continue with the head.

HEAD

Round 32: Change to **skin** colour, 2 sc in each st. (24 sts)

Round 33: *3 sc, 2 sc in the next st, rep from * to end. (30 sts)

Stuff the neck area firmly at this point.

Round 34: *4 sc, 2 sc in the next st, rep from * to end. (36 sts)

Round 35: *5 sc, 2 sc in the next st, rep from * to end. (42 sts)

Round 36: 1 sc in each st.

Round 37: 26 sc, 1 bobble st for the nose *(see Stitches: Bobble st)*, 1 sc in each st to end. Be sure to align the nose with the middle of the legs and adjust the positioning if necessary.

Rounds 38 to 46: 1 sc in each st.

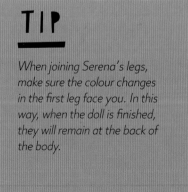

TIP

When joining Serena's legs, make sure the colour changes in the first leg face you. In this way, when the doll is finished, they will remain at the back of the body.

Round 47: *5 sc, sc2tog, rep from * to end. (36 sts)

Start stuffing the head at this point.

Round 48: *4 sc, sc2tog, rep from * to end. (30 sts)

Place safety eyes one round above the nose, with 8 sts between them, embroider cheeks with **pink** yarn.

Round 49: *3 sc, sc2tog, rep from * to end. (24 sts)

Round 50: *2 sc, sc2tog, rep from * to end. (18 sts)

Stuff firmly.

Round 51: *1 sc, sc2tog, rep from * to end. (12 sts)

Round 52: (sc2tog) 6 times. (6 sts)

Fasten off and weave in ends.

TENNIS SUIT SKIRT

Turn the body upside down and join **light purple** yarn in one of the front loops of round 18, at the back of the body.

Round 1: 1 sc FLO in each st of round 18. (30 sts)

Round 2: *4 sc, 2 sc in the next st, rep from * to end. (36 sts)

Round 3: 1 sc in each st.

Round 4: *5 sc, 2 sc in the next st, rep from * to end. (42 sts)

Round 5: 1 sc in each st.

Round 6: *6 sc, 2 sc in the next st, rep from * to end. (48 sts)

Round 7: 1 sc in each st.

Fasten off and weave in ends.

ARMS (MAKE TWO)

Round 1: Using **skin** colour, ch 2, 4 sc in the second ch from hook. (4 sts)

Round 2: 2 sc in each st. (8 sts)

Rounds 3 to 5: 1 sc in each st.

Round 6: Change to **light purple** yarn, 1 sc BLO in each st.

There is no need to stuff the arms.

Rounds 7 to 16: 1 sc in each st.

Round 17: Press the opening with your fingers, aligning 4 sts side by side and sc both sides together by working 1 sc into each pair of sts *(see Techniques: Closing the Arms)*.

Fasten off, leaving a long tail to sew to the body.

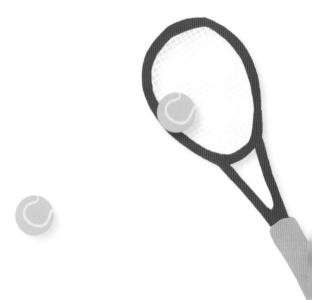

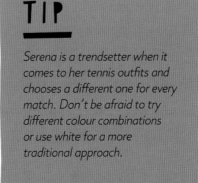

TIP

Serena is a trendsetter when it comes to her tennis outfits and chooses a different one for every match. Don't be afraid to try different colour combinations or use white for a more traditional approach.

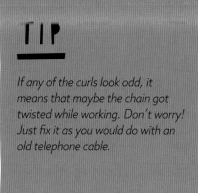

TIP

If any of the curls look odd, it means that maybe the chain got twisted while working. Don't worry! Just fix it as you would do with an old telephone cable.

HAIR

Round 1: Using **black** for the hair, 6 sc in a magic ring. (6 sts)

Round 2: 2 sc in each st. (12 sts)

Round 3: *1 sc, 2 sc in the next st, rep from * to end. (18 sts)

Round 4: *2 sc, 2 sc in the next st, rep from * to end. (24 sts)

Round 5: *3 sc, 2 sc in the next st, rep from * to end. (30 sts)

Round 6: *4 sc, 2 sc in the next st, rep from * to end. (36 sts)

Round 7: *5 sc, 2 sc in the next st, rep from * to end. (42 sts)

Round 8: *13 sc, 2 sc in the next st, rep from * to end. (45 sts)

Rounds 9 to 17: 1 sc in each st.

Fasten off, leaving a long tail to sew to the head.

PONYTAIL

Round 1: Using **black** for the hair, 6 sc in a magic ring. (6 sts)

Round 2: 2 sc in each st. (12 sts)

Round 3: *ch 41, 3 sc in the second ch from hook, 3 sc in each st along ch (120 sts), 2 sc BLO, rep from * 6 times (6 hair locks)

Fasten off, leaving a long tail to sew to the head.

"It's all about, for me, how you recover. I think I've always said a champion isn't about how much they win, but it's about how they recover from their downs, whether it's an injury or whether it's a loss."

HEADBAND

The headband is crocheted in rows.

Row 1: Using **light purple** yarn, ch 5, 1 sc in the second ch from hook, 1 sc in each ch to end. (4 sts)

Rows 2 to 55: Ch 1, turn, 1 sc BLO in each st.

Row 56: Measure the headband against the head of your Serena and adjust the length by adding or subtracting a row or two. Once you are satisfied with its length, join both ends, to form a circle: ch 1, 1 slst each back loop of the last row with 1 remaining loop of the foundation chain (4 slst).

Fasten off and weave in ends.

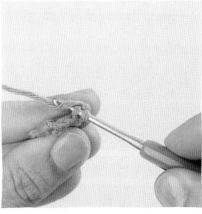

ASSEMBLY

Sew the hair to the head *(see Techniques: Sewing the Hair)*.

Sew the ponytail to the top of Serena's head, wrong side of the piece pointing up and use the remaining front loops of round 3 to work the stitches with your yarn needle in and out. Tie the hair locks together with a bit of **light purple** yarn.

Sew the arms to the sides of the body *(see Techniques: Sewing the Arms)*.

Place the headband around her forehead.

Weave in all ends inside the doll.

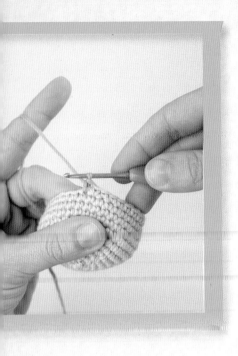

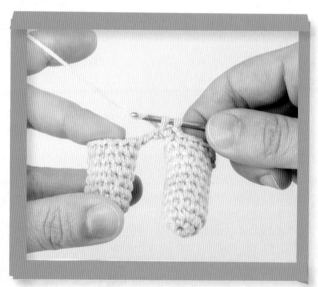

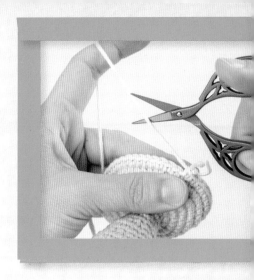

TECHNIQUES
AND TUTORIALS

Here you will find all of the techniques and tutorials that you need to
create your dolls and their accessories. I have included an explanation
for each technique, along with lots of photos, so that you can follow
them easily. You may prefer to use your own methods, and that's fine
too, but they're here if you need them and I hope they help you with the
placement of your hook or stitches and to sew your dolls together.

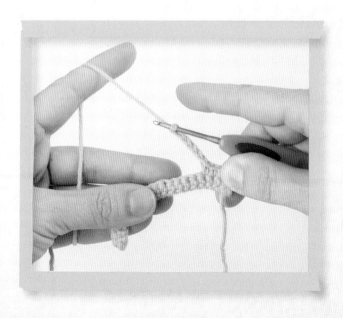

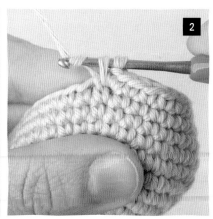

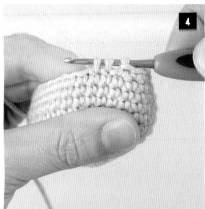

TIP

An invisible single crochet decreases can be used to make your decreasing less visible by working into the front loops only of the stitches being worked.

ANATOMY OF A STITCH

Every finished stitch looks like a sideways letter **v**, with two loops meeting at one end (**1**). The loop closer to you is the **front loop** and the loop behind it is the **back loop**. You will sometimes be asked to crochet certain stitches in the front loops (FLO) or in the back loops (BLO) only and there's always a reason for this: you will use the remaining loops later!

INCREASING

This means working two stitches in one same stitch (**2**). After you have worked the first stitch, you simply insert your hook back into the same place and work the next stitch.

INVISIBLE SINGLE CROCHET DECREASE

A crochet decrease means working two stitches together at the same time, so that it goes unnoticed. Insert the hook in the front loop of the next stitch (**3**) and in the front loop of the stitch next to that, one at a time (**4**). Yarn over hook and draw it through both front loops in one go. Yarn over hook again and draw it through the two remaining loops on your hook (**5**).

REGULAR SINGLE CROCHET DECREASE

Some projects in this book, like the hood of Greta's hoodie, use a regular single crochet decrease which is worked just the same as an invisible single crochet decrease, but you insert your hook under both loops of the stitches.

CHANGING COLOUR

To change to another colour you should join the new colour during the final step of the last stitch in the previous colour. This means that when the last two loops of the stitch remain on your hook (**1**), you should grab the new colour, wrap it around your hook (**2**) and pull it through those two loops. This will leave the new colour on your hook (**3**), ready to work the next stitch in that colour (**4**).

When working pieces that will be stuffed later, I cut the yarn of the old colour and tie this into a knot with the new colour, inside of the piece, to secure both tails. This can only be done in three-dimensional pieces, of course, because these knots will remain inside the doll and won't be visible. When working flat pieces, that have a right and wrong side, you will have to weave in the ends in between the stitches in the wrong side.

FASTEN OFF INVISIBLY

This method avoids the little stub that can look unsightly when you fasten off your crochet. When you have your final loop on hook and have finished your crochet, cut yarn, take yarn over hook and pull all the way through final loop. Pull yarn tight, which creates a small knot. Thread yarn tail onto tapestry needle and insert needle, from back of work, underneath the top **v** of second stitch along the main edge (**5**). Pull yarn all the way through. Insert needle from front, into the top **v** of the last stitch made and pull yarn through (**6**). You have created a 'mimic' stitch that covers the small knot and joins up the round neatly.

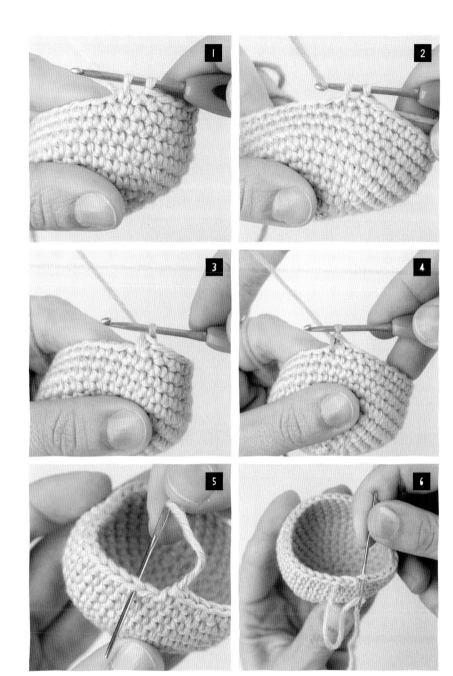

TIP

All the dolls are worked in rounds, in a continuous spiral, so it's essential to use a stitch marker to help identify the beginning of each round. Move the stitch marker up as you work.

CLOSING REMAINING STITCHES THROUGH THE FRONT LOOPS

After the final round, you may be instructed to close the remaining stitches through the front loops. To do this, fasten off after last stitch and thread yarn onto a tapestry needle. Insert needle through each visible loop of the last round of stitches (through one loop of stitch only) (**1**). When you reach the end, pull gently to close up the gap (**2**). Secure the thread with a few stitches and hide the ends inside the doll.

HIDING ENDS INSIDE THE DOLL

Insert your crochet hook into the doll, in between stitches, a few centimetres (a couple of inches) from the tail end that you want to hide, then push the hook out between stitches that are close to the tail end, and making sure that the hook is really close to the tail end of yarn (**3**). Take yarn over hook and pull through the doll and as you pull out your hook, the yarn will come with it. Snip the yarn close to the doll to leave a clean finish (**4**).

WORKING IN ROWS

Flat pieces are worked in rows, starting with a foundation chain. This is a string of chain stitches. It's important not to twist the chain, so keep a tight grip on the crocheted chains near your hook.

WORKING IN ROUNDS

All the dolls in this book have the same body structure and they are worked in rounds, in a continuous spiral, so there's no need to close the round after finishing each one of them. This is why the use of stitch markers is of the essence. It's important to mark the beginning of each round with a stitch marker and move this stitch marker up as you work.

MAGIC RING

Round pieces always start with a magic ring, because, when tightened, it will have no holes in the middle where stuffing could come out. To make a magic ring, start in the same way that you would a slip knot, by making a loop shape with the tail end of the yarn. Insert the hook into it and draw another loop of yarn through it. But do not pull the tail end. As well as the loop on your hook, you will have a large loop sitting beneath your hook, with a twisted section of yarn (**1**). It is important that you work into the centre of the loop for your first round, and also that you work over the twisted section of yarn (**2**). When you have completed your first round, you can pull the yarn tail tight to close the hole (**3**).

JOINING LEGS

You will always start the dolls in this book by crocheting the legs, which need to be joined, to continue then with the body up to the head.

You will crochet one leg first and set it aside while you crochet the second leg. Then, with leg 2 still on your hook, you will chain 3 to join leg 1 with a sc (**4**). This will be the new beginning of the following rounds, so it's important to place a stitch marker there. You will then have to crochet a further 11 sc all along leg 1 and, after that, crochet 3 sc in one of the sides of the 3-ch-loop (**5**). Then, crochet 12 sc along leg 2 (**6**) so you can finally work 3 sc on the other side of the 3-ch-loop (**7**). You will end up with a round of 30 stitches which will be the beginning of the body of your doll.

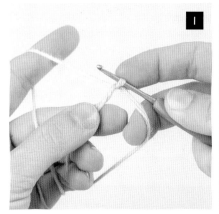
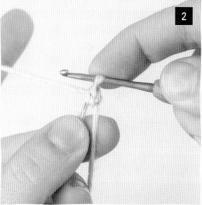

TIP

You may need to practise a magic ring a few times before you feel totally comfortable with the technique, but if you can persevere and master it, the start of your crochet will be really neat.

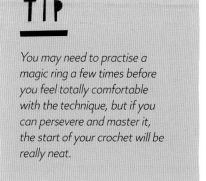

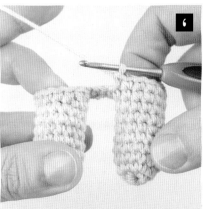

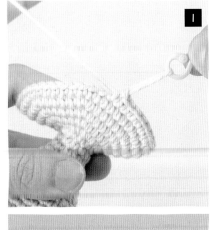

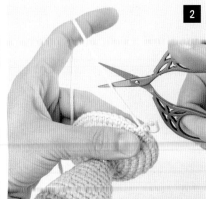

TIP

For safety reasons, if you are crocheting the doll for a small child, you should embroider the eyes with **black** *or* **dark brown** *leftover pieces of yarn instead of using toy safety eyes.*

INTERRUPTING YOUR WORK

Sometimes I will recommend you to stop crocheting the head at some point before finishing, either to crochet a coat or collar without having the stuffed head interfering the movements of your hands. To do this, you can place a stitch marker on the loop on your hook, so the stitches won't come off (**1**). Then you can cut the yarn (**2**). When you are ready, you can join the yarn again as you would do for a colour change.

ATTACHING EYES

Safety eyes have two parts: the front with a straight or threaded rod, and a washer that goes inside the toy. If fastened correctly, it's almost impossible to remove them. But beware, if you are crocheting the doll for a small child, you should probably consider embroidering them with **black** or **dark brown** leftover pieces of yarn.

SEWING THE CHEEKS

These are made whilst the head is in progress, after you have attached the safety eyes (if using). Use a short length of **pink** yarn and thread onto a tapestry needle. Working from the inside of the head, in line with lower edge of eye and a few stitches away, make a small running stitch over one or two stitches, either straight (**3**) or on a diagonal (**4**), bringing needle back through to inside of head. Tie off ends.

CREATING THE V COLLAR

Place a stitch marker in the loop on your hook to secure. Join yarn 2 rounds below the tip of the skin triangle (**1**). Working in the spaces between sts, surface sc 2 sts which will take you to the tip of the skin coloured triangle. Now follow the diagonal of the triangle, working the right side first. Crochet 1 surface sc in between each round, inserting the hook in the spaces between rounds, until you reach the round where the front loops at the neck are showing (**2**). Now crochet 2 sc in each front loop of the shirt bordering the doll's neck, until you reach the edge of the triangle on the other side. Work 5 surface sc in between rounds following the diagonal of the triangle to the starting stitch, work 1 slst in the starting stitch (**3**). Fasten off and weave in ends (**4**).

WEAVING IN ENDS

With the wrong side of your piece facing, thread tail end onto a tapestry needle and insert the needle underneath the posts of three or four stitches (**5**). Pull yarn through and snip close to work (**6**). If you feel it necessary you can repeat this process by working back through the same stitches: skip the first stitch and then insert your needle underneath the next few stitches. Pull yarn through and snip yarn close to work.

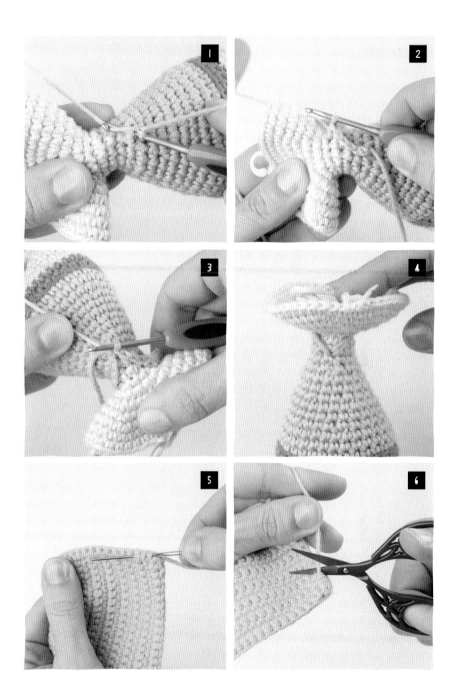

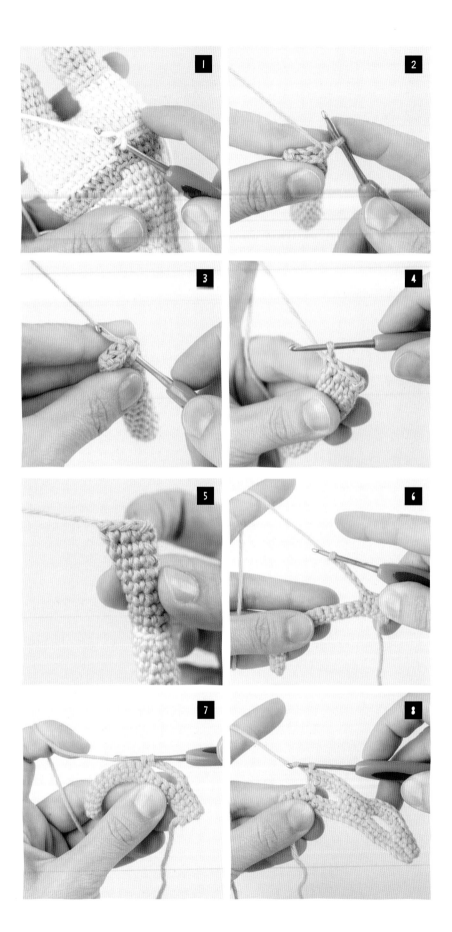

JOINING THE YARN TO BEGIN A SKIRT

Some details that build the wardrobe of these characters, like skirts, are crocheted to the body of the doll and are not removable. To this end you will always find that the pattern calls for a special round where you will work into the remaining front loops in the body of your doll.

To join in the yarn to create a skirt, t-shirt, coat or collar, you will always need to hold your doll's head down (even if the head is not quite finished) and look for the remaining front loop right in the middle of the back of your doll. I usually pick the last front loop of the round (which is next to the first front loop of the round) and join my yarn right there and then crochet towards the left (**1**).

CLOSING THE ARMS

The arms of the dolls look like crochet tubes and they do not need to be filled with stuffing. In the last round you will be asked to close the tube by flattening the opening, so that 4 stitches of the top layer become aligned with 4 stitches of the lower layer (**2**). Once you've achieved this, join both layers by crocheting 1 sc in each pair of stitches (**3**). You will end up with 4 sc (**4**). Fasten off but remember to leave a long yarn tail to sew to the body (**5**).

CREATING ARMHOLES ON VESTS

Armholes are created over two rows, and full instructions are included for each doll's vest. On the first row, you make a chain of stitches (**6**) then skip as many stitches as indicated before working the next sc (**7**). This creates a chain loop which is the gap for the armhole. On the next row, you work stitches into the chain loops (**8**) and the armholes are complete.

EDGING OF FLAT PIECES

Many of the flat pieces have a crocheted edge to create a neat finish. To do this, you will work as many stitches as instructed in the pattern, working either along the edge and inserting your hook in between the spaces between rows (**1**), or into stitches themselves (**2**), depending on which edge you are working along.

SEWING THE ARMS

Thread yarn tail onto a tapestry needle and place the arm against the side of the body. When you are happy with placement insert the needle through a stitch on the body (**3**), pull yarn through. Insert needle through the top of the next stitch on the arm (**4**), pull yarn through. Repeat this process until the arm is sewn in place (**5**). Secure yarn with a few stitches and follow the instructions for hiding the ends inside the doll.

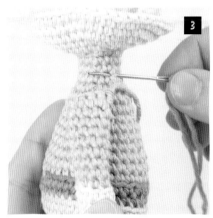

TIP

I usually sew the arms to the dolls between rounds 28 and 29 of the body. But this is up to you. If the doll has a collar, remember to lift it a bit before sewing!

TIP

The hair locks will tend to curl naturally as you go, but if they don't, you can help them with your fingers, by twisting them into shape like a corkscrew.

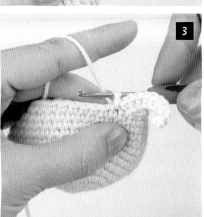

CROCHETING CURLS

Many of the dolls in this book have curls, some of them are short, like Queen Elizabeth's and Florence Nightingale's and some of them are longer like Malala's. All these curls start with a foundation chain (the length of which will be indicated in the pattern), working from the hair cap (**1**) and then you will have to crochet 1 sc in each back loop of each chain stitch (**2**) until you reach the edge of the hair piece again (**3**). Do not use the back bumps of the foundation chain unless specified. These hair locks will tend to curl naturally as you go, but if they don't, help them with your fingers, twisting them into shape.

SEWING THE HAIR

Use small straight stitches to sew the hair to the head, working over the sc stitches of the hair (**4**) and making sure that you also work through the stitches of the head, to join them securely. It's OK to space the stitches out as you don't need to work through over every stitch (**5**). Don't pull yarn too tightly when sewing, otherwise your stitches may distort the shape of the head. Use matching coloured yarn so that these stitches are not visible.

SEWING LOOSE PIECES

If required, stuff the piece to be sewn. Thread the tapestry needle and position the piece in place. Secure it with pins. Do you like it there? Then let's go! Using backstitching, sew the piece with your needle going through under both loops of the last round.

FLOWERS

First you will work the first round of 5dc into a magic ring as instructed in the pattern.

Work one slip stitch in the next stitch, chain two (**1**).

Yarn over hook, insert the hook back into the same stitch, yarn over hook and pull yarn through the stitch (**2**).

Yarn over hook, pull yarn through two loops on your hook (**3**).

Yarn over hook, insert hook into the same stitch, yarn over hook and pull yarn through the stitch (**4**).

Yarn over hook, pull yarn through the first two loops on your hook (**5**).

Yarn over hook, pull yarn through the three remaining loops on your hook, chain two (**6**).

Work one slip stitch in the same stitch (**7**).

Repeat steps 1 to 7 a further 4 times to make 5 petals; finish with a slip stitch in the next stitch. Make as many flowers as instructed (**8**).

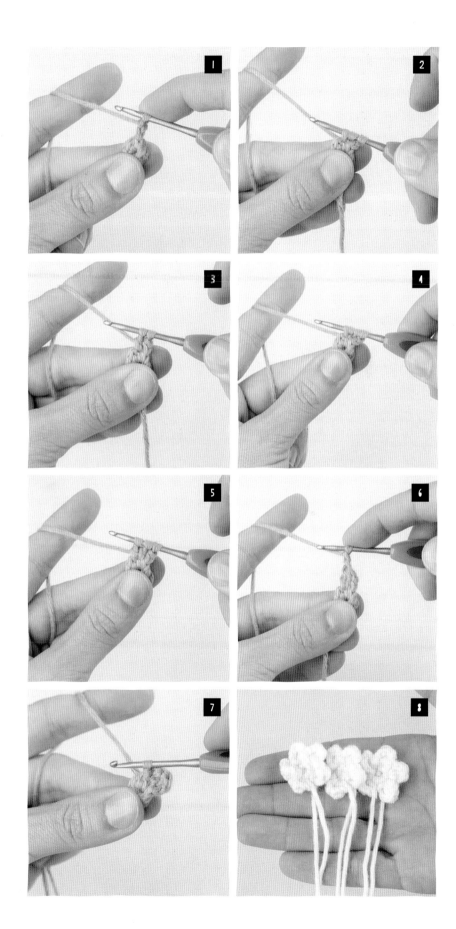

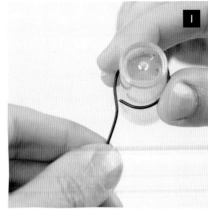

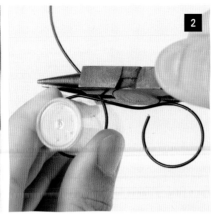

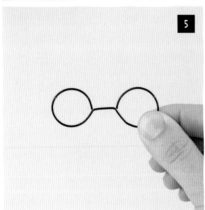

TIP

Once you have made your glasses, you can attach them onto the nose of your doll using craft glue or small stitches to hold them in place.

MAKING GLASSES

Some of the dolls wear glasses and here is the best way to make them.

First, take a small plastic lid or tube, approximately 1cm (⅜in) in diameter. Wrap your wire around the lid fully, to create the first lens and bend the wire away slightly where it meets to start forming the bridge for the nose (**1**)

Leave approximately 1cm (⅜in) of straight wire for the bridge and then wrap the wire around the plastic lid or tube again, to create the second lens. (**2**).

Snip the wire where the second lens meets (**3**).

Use the pliers to close up the gaps as much as possible where the wires meet and to complete your glasses (**4** and **5**).

SOME ADDITIONAL NOTES

The bodies of these dolls, and most of their hair features and accessories, are crocheted by working in a spiral. Remember to mark the beginning of each round with a stitch marker. No need to close each round with a slip stitch.

When changing colours, you'll get a "step" in the fabric and yes, we all hate it. There is no way to avoid it, so embrace it and try to place it at the back of your dolls!

I usually use bits of **pink** yarn to embroider the cheeks of the dolls. But you can also opt for fabric blushes or markers!

Can I wash these dolls? Yes, you can! If you only want to remove a small stain, just dampen the area with a wet cloth and a bit of soap. If you want to wash the doll completely, place it in the washing machine: gentle cycle and tumble dry low. Warning: some colours might fade just a bit.

MAKE YOUR OWN ICON

I hope that I've now inspired you to get creative and make your own crocheted icon. You can mix and match outfits, make hair curls longer or shorter and change the colours or skin tones to create your own special icons.

ABOUT THE AUTHOR

Hello! I'm Carla and I live in Buenos Aires, Argentina.

I am sure it comes as no surprise that I am a doll lover. I have always loved dolls and still buy them for myself although I'm in my forties! Learning to crochet and be able to make them myself has been a turning point in my life. I have always been rather crafty, but nothing has given me the joy and satisfaction of crocheting. It is my best possible therapy.

And it's also my secret power. Because in the real world, the one inhabited by humans, I'm a journalist and the producer of a TV talk show on National Politics and almost no one in my workplace knows of my secret identity as a doll designer. I love being part of two such different worlds.

I am also the mother of two very energetic and mischievous boys, both redheads, so I am basically a night-crocheter: when it's dark outside and everything is quiet, I make myself a cup of tea and let all my worries go between yarns and hooks!

ACKNOWLEDGEMENTS

Thank you so much my dear friends and followers for supporting my designs, for your beautiful comments and amazing feedback. This book is for you!

Sarah Callard, you are my fairy godmother! Thank you so much for making my dream come true!

I want to thank Sam Staddon for her wonderful design and Jason Jenkins for the incredible photos in this book, but mostly I will be eternally grateful to them for the two amazing days of photoshooting in Tunbridge Wells, Kent. Thanks for driving me around, for your never-ending patience, for dinner and for our lovely chats. Meeting you was one of the best things this book has gifted me!

Dear Lynne Rowe, thank you for your guidance and help. I couldn't have done it without you! And I also want to thank Jessica Cropper, Anna Wade and everyone at David & Charles: this has been the ride of a lifetime.

My mother always warned me that, if I ever won an Academy Award, I should thank her. Well, Mom, this is my Oscar. Thank you for being my best and most honest critic and supporter and for providing endless quantities of pillow stuffing for my dolls (where do you get them from?). Thanks to my father for finding everything I do just perfect and giving me confidence every step of the way. Thanks to my brother and sister-in-law for letting me stay at their home in London and for hoarding the yarn balls I compulsively buy online. Thank you also for giving me two beautiful nieces to whom I hope to inspire with all these incredible icons.

But most of all a huge thanks to my beloved husband, for keeping the children busy so I could bring these dolls to life, for sharing a house with me where dolls just pop out from everywhere (yep, the kitchen too) and for enduring hours of driving with me, silent by your side, because... I'm counting stitches! This was all possible because of you.

INDEX

As the publisher, we want to honour the struggles experienced by many of the women featured in this collection by supporting a charity that works to empower girls through education.

We are happy to announce that 5% of the receipts from this book will be donated to WONDER foundation, a woman-led non-profit organisation dedicated to transforming the lives of women, girls and their communities through access to quality education.

WONDER was established as a charity in 2012 as the Women's Network for Development and Educational Resources (WONDER), with a drive to empowering vulnerable people through education.

Their Vision

WONDER is working towards a future where women and girls are empowered to make informed life choices and lead the way in their own personal development.

Their Mission

To empower women, girls and their community through access to quality education so that they can exit poverty for good.

Find out more at **www.wonderfoundation.org.uk**

A DAVID AND CHARLES BOOK
© David and Charles, Ltd 2020

David and Charles is an imprint of David and Charles, Ltd
Suite A, Tourism House, Pynes Hill, Exeter, EX2 5WS

Text and Designs © CARLA MITRANI 2020
Layout and Photography © David and Charles, Ltd 2020

First published in the UK and USA in 2020

A catalogue record for this book is available from the British Library.

ISBN-13: 9781446308257 paperback
ISBN-13: 9781446379806 EPUB
ISBN-13: 9781446381595 PDF

Printed in China through Asia Pacific Offset for:
David and Charles, Ltd
Suite A, Tourism House, Pynes Hill, Exeter, EX2 5WS

10 9 8 7 6 5

Senior Commissioning Editor: Sarah Callard
Managing Editor: Jessica Cropper
Project Editor: Lynne Rowe
Head of Design: Anna Wade
Design and Art Direction: Sam Staddon
Illustrator: Prudence Rogers
Photographer: Jason Jenkins
Pre-Press Designer: Ali Stark
Production Manager: Beverley Richardson

David and Charles publishes high-quality books on a wide range of subjects. For more information visit www.davidandcharles.com.

Share your makes with us on social media using #dandcbooks and follow us on Facebook and Instagram by searching for @dandcbooks.

Layout of the digital edition of this book may vary depending on reader hardware and display settings.